A Practical Guide to
Understanding Gender Variance
including
Transgender, Intersex, Non-Binary & Gender Fluid Individuals

3rd Edition (2023)

All rights reserved. No part of this publication may be reproduced or transmitted in any form or by any means, electronic, mechanical, including photocopying, recording or by any information storage retrieval system without permission from the author.

The right of Helen Dale to be identified as the author of this work has been asserted by her in accordance with the Copyright, Designs and Patents Act 1988

All trademarks are acknowledged as belonging to the relevant organisations

© Helen Dale 2018, 2023
ISBN 978-1-7397667-4-0

About the Author

Helen Dale is a woman with a trans history. She has been actively involved in the trans community – as counsellor, chair of several trans and LGBT organisations and trainer and more recently as an author – for more than twenty-five years. She lives in Salford, England.

Her early career was in Public Relations, Advertising and Marketing then IT support. She was the first openly transgender employee nationally in the UK Probation Service in 1999.

She served on national and local Diversity Boards within Probation and National Offender Management Service and received a number of awards for work with transgender individuals, including the Butler Trust Award presented by HRH Princess Royal, Princess Anne, at Buckingham Palace. She was also made an Honorary Life Member of a:gender — the pan Civil Service trans support network.

She developed a trans awareness workshop as part of her Diploma in Counselling course in 2001; this was then adapted for different audiences and updated to reflect changing circumstances. It continues to receive positive feedback. This Guide is based on those workshops.

Since retiring in 2015, she has been a volunteer with Diversity Role Models and facilitated sessions in primary and secondary schools dealing with homophobic, biphobic and transphobic bullying. She has also continued counselling transgender clients and has written a number of books.

Contents

Chapter 1 Introduction 1
Why this book? 1
Introduction to Transgender Issues and Expectations 1
Use of 'Transsexual' and 'Transvestite' v 'Transgender' 1
My Experience 2
Dissatisfaction with Counsellors' Experience 2
Reinforcing Stereotypes 2
Who this Book is For 3
Sources of Information 3

Chapter 2 Definitions 5
What does 'Transgender' mean? 5
Trans and Intersex Labels: 5
Other Related Terms 11
Other Abbreviations used in this Guide 12

Chapter 3 Causality 13
Gender Variations 13
Nurture v Nature 13
What is the difference between Male and Female Brains? 14
Transgender Continuum 18
TG Drive v Braking Force 19

Chapter 4 Social Transition 21
Deciding to Transition 21
Legal Protection 22
Changing Names (different rules apply in Scotland) 22
Changing Names in Scotland 22
Impact of Transition on Relationships 22
Gender Stereotypes 23
Avoiding Attention in Public 23
Non-Binary / Gender Fluid Social Transition 24

Chapter 5 Myth Busting 25
Myth No 1: Sex = Gender 25
Myth No 2: Sex is Binary 25
Myth No 3: Chromosomes XX = Female, XY= Male 25
Myth No 4: Sex Can't Change 26
Myth No 5: Transvestism is a fetish 26
Myth No 6: All Transgender People have Surgery 26
Myth No 7: Trans = Gay 27
Myth No 8: Trans Women are a Threat 27
Young People 27
Myth No 9: It's a Fad/ They are Attention Seeking 27
Myth No 10: They are Too Young to Know 27
Myth No 11: Exposed to Irreversible Changes 28

Chapter 6 Transsexual Journey to Surgery 29
WPATH Standards of Care 29
NHS Gender Identity Clinics or Private 29
Adults 29

Contents

 Young People 30
 Private Providers 30
 Real Life Experience (Real Life Test) 30
 Hormone Treatment 31
 Electrolysis 31
 Speech Therapy 31
 Referral for surgery 31
 Male-to-female Surgical Procedures 31
 Female-to-Male Surgical Procedures 32
 Time Off for Treatment 32
 Preparing for Surgery 33
 Recovering from Surgery 33
 Young Trans People 34

Chapter 7 Travelling On: Post Transition/ Surgery 35
 8 Stage Process as a Trans Person 35
 To be Out or Not? 36
 Passing/ Stealth 36
 Relationships 36
 Cross Gender Health Risks 37

Chapter 8 Trans Issues in Counselling 39
 Who am I? 39
 What do I do about being trans? What if I don't do anything? 40
 What are the consequences of transition? 40
 Transition 41
 Medical complications 41
 Self Esteem 43
 Self-harm & Suicide 43
 Relationships 43
 Lack of understanding 44
 Post Transition 44
 Coming Out 45
 Remaining Stealth 45
 Sexuality Issues 45
 Isolation/ support 45
 Issues from upbringing 46
 Employment 46
 Other 46
 Special Issues 46
 Therapeutic Approaches: Holistic and Eclectic 48

Chapter 9 Partners and Families 49
 Partner/Husband/ Wife/Spouse: 49
 Children 50
 Siblings 50
 Parents 50

Chapter 10 Case Studies 52
 A 52
 B 54
 C 54
 D 54

E 54
F 55

Chapter 11 Legal history 56

P v S & Cornwall County Council 1996 56
Sex Discrimination Act — Gender Reassignment Regulations 1998 56
Gender Recognition Act 2004 56
Goods & Services 2008 58
Civil Partnership 2004 & Marriage (Same Sex Couples) Act 2013 58
Equality Act 2010 58

Chapter 12 Discrimination and Hate Crime/ Incidents 60

Jokes 60
Abuse 60
Physical Assaults 61
Criminal damage 61
Sporting 61
Media Portrayal 61
Goods & Services 61
At Work 62
Changing Documents 62
Schools 63
Family 63

Chapter 13 Employment 64

Diversity Benefits Business 64
Monitoring Gender & Gender Identity 65
Single-sex facilities 65
Non-binary / gender-fluid 65
Support for the Individual 66
Transitioning In Service 66
Existing records that can't be changed 68
New applicants 68
Harassment 70
Medical Adjustments/ Absences 71
Surgery 72
Performance issues 72
Transgender Awareness Training 72

Chapter 14 Bibliography 73

Risks Myths and Sexuality 73
True Selves 73
As Nature Made Him 73
Transgender Warriors 73
The Transgender Debate 73
Brainsex 74
Stand-Up for Yourself 74
True Colours 74
Trans Britain 74
Trans Mental Health Study 2012 74
Tale of Two Lives 75
Transgender Tales 75

Contents

Chapter 15 Appendices 76

    Appendix 1.   Gender Recognition Act 2004 Section 22 76
    Appendix 2.   Statutory Instrument 2005-635................................ 78
    Appendix 3.   Transition Check list... 82
    Appendix 4.   Disclosure Agreement.. 86
    Appendix 5.   Brain Quadrant Test... 88

Also by Helen Dale 91

    A Tale of Two Lives... 91
    Transgender Tales 92
    Summer Dreams 93
    Changes 94
    Impact 94
    Imposter 95
    Operation Busted Flush 95

Chapter 1 Introduction

Why this book?

Introduction to Transgender Issues and Expectations

In 2001, while I was studying for my Diploma in Counselling, we were set an assignment to look at the 'Counselling Needs and Issues' facing a specific sector of the community. Not surprisingly, I chose male-to-female transsexual individuals in the UK. I tried to find existing information in this field and was able to locate very little. What was available seemed to consider transgender issues mainly from the perspective of sexuality — and whilst there are significant overlaps, this seemed to me to be flawed.

At the time, I only found one book that I considered presented any sound advice for those dealing with transgendered individuals — **Risks, Myths and Sexuality** edited by Paul Head.

Since then, a couple of further very useful books *have* been written and I particularly commend *Gender Loving Care* — although a significant section of the information is specific to the USA. I also recommend Shelley Bridgman's **Stand-Up for Yourself** — one of the best autobiographies I've read by a trans person and an excellent insight into what it means coming to terms with being trans and the subsequent process. *True Colours* by Caroline Paige — the first openly transgender officer serving in the British military also gives an excellent account. I hope, however, to be able to extend the range of information available to those dealing with transgendered individuals, especially in the UK. I hope, too, that my own autobiography *A Tale of Two Lives — a Funny Thing Happened on the Way to the Palace* will also contribute to understanding trans people.

Perhaps my perspective of having been through the process myself and of having chatted to trans individuals when they could be totally honest with their thoughts allows me to dispel some of the myths that have developed regarding trans.

Use of 'Transsexual' and 'Transvestite' v 'Transgender'

I am aware that the terms 'transsexual' and 'transvestite' have fallen out of favour with many trans individuals and there is a tendency to use 'transgender' instead. However, this book sometimes needs to differentiate between an individual who feels the need to transition (transsexual) and others who cross-dress but have no intention of permanently and completely changing (transvestite). It is also true to say that a significant part of the community considers the term 'transsexual' to be more accurate than 'transgender' – on the basis that they don't change their gender, they alter their sexual characteristics. I will, therefore, use the terms 'transsexual' and 'transvestite' to differentiate when appropriate and 'trans' as an umbrella term.

Chapter 1 Introduction

My Experience

I spent decades 'cross-dressing', as I saw it, before I accepted that I was transsexual rather than transvestite. I went through long periods of denial or suppression. I didn't even know there was a word for what I did until my late teens when I had moved to London and found a magazine in a bookshop in Soho showing that I wasn't the only one in the world.

When I first moved to Salford in 1997, my flat was a haven for transvestites and transsexual individuals and I lost count of the number that stopped over to go out in Manchester's' Gay Village. We would then come back at about 2, 3 or 4 am and sit talking for hours, drinking coffee and eating French bread, ham and mature English Cheddar as the sun eventually rose over Salford. There was no reason not to be open about our feelings and our doubts, no axes to grind, no one to impress.

Since then, I've counselled scores of gender variant individuals, I've met transsexual prisoners serving sentences for manslaughter, murder and arson and lesser offences. I've chatted to well over a thousand trans individuals (and I don't just mean 'hi, how are you?'); belonged to a number of internet message groups, Facebook groups etc. and estimate that over the last twenty years or so I've seen more than half a million messages. Even if only 1% of those were significant, that's still 5,000 relevant messages.

I also had some questionnaires on the internet aimed at transsexual people, transvestites and the general public. Some 300 of the responses were analysed for my original Diploma in Counselling assignment. The responses I received have been verified over the years by individuals in face-to-face conversations.

Dissatisfaction with Counsellors' Experience

One of the key facts to emerge from those questionnaires was the level of dissatisfaction of transsexual people with counselling they had received — yet nearly all of them said they thought counselling was of value to trans people. The major issue was the lack of awareness of trans issues by most counsellors. This remains the case even 25 years later.

Reinforcing Stereotypes

So many individuals, attending Gender Identity Clinics, even just a few years ago, felt obliged to tell the psychiatrists what they thought they wanted to hear just to ensure treatment. This, of course, simply reinforced stereotypes. With a perception that you HAD to be totally convinced you were transsexual to obtain treatment — and that if you expressed the slightest doubts your treatment would be terminated — is it any wonder that such doubts were never expressed?

The reality is that the vast majority of transsexual people DO question if they are doing the right thing at some stage of their process. In fact, I'd suggest that those who do not question what they are doing simply cannot understand the gravity of the step that they are taking.

This book deals with issues facing individuals who are intersex, transsexual or transvestite or otherwise fall within the umbrella of 'transgender'. I acknowledge that the use of some of these terms and the inclusion of some of those 'categories' does not meet with universal approval of those that might fall within this remit. Some of these terms change over the years or are interpreted differently. Much of it relates to individuals who transition from one gender to another — or present as a different gender. I also try to look at the increasingly significant numbers of individuals who do not fit into a binary classification of genders, some whose gender identity fluctuates and those who don't identify as a particular gender.

Who this Book is For

This book is aimed at anyone dealing with trans individuals whether as carer, counsellor, therapist, nurse, doctor, teacher or lecturer, personnel officer, line manager or subordinate, colleague, offender manager or supervisor, prison or police officer, magistrate or judge or friend and, hopefully, those who are gender variant themselves.

The book has been in production for a number of years. In the meantime, there have been major changes: the Gender Recognition Act 2004, the Civil Partnership Act 2004, the Equality Acts 2006 and 2010 and the requirement for Gender Equality Duties to include trans individuals. As I wrote in 2021, the Gender Recognition Act was due to be reviewed with a view to extending its remit and simplifying the process for changing one's legal gender. Update 2023: after possibly the most comprehensive review of any proposed legislation, the conclusion was that the changes should be made. Indeed, the conservative government, under Theresa May, promised to do so. Then Boris Johnson took over and the plans were fudged then dropped. In 2023, Prime Minister Rishi Sunak made a statement at the Conservative Party conference in Manchester that "A man is a man, and a woman is a woman" and "we shouldn't be bullied into believing that people can be any sex they want to be – they can't." The Health Secretary, Stephen Barclay, proposed that transgender women will be banned from being treated in female hospital wards in England."

Following a single case involving a prisoner claiming to be transgender, HMPPS revised their policy on managing transgender offenders. I have, therefore, removed the section of this book dealing with prisons.

Although it is aimed at various professional groups and trans people themselves, I hope to avoid technical terms and jargon or, where this is unavoidable, to explain the relevant terms. I hope the book will be readable — and entertaining at times.

Sources of Information

I've taken information from various sources particularly material produced by **Press for Change** (the campaigning group for transsexual people), **GIRES**, **a:gender** — the Pan-Civil Service Trans and Intersex support network, and the **Trans Mental Health Study 2012** to support my own experience and views. Special thanks to Karen Harvey for the information on Intersex.

My experience has been gained from:

- 50+ years identifying as transvestite (even when I was unaware that the word existed) followed by my own transition process and treatment in the mid/late 1990s leading to surgery in November 2000.
- Acting as a consultant on transgender issues for National Probation Service (NPS) Greater Manchester Probation Trust and other Probation Trusts

Chapter 1 Introduction

regarding 12 offenders and representing LGB&T perspectives on national diversity groups

- Acting as a consultant to other areas where colleagues have transitioned at work
- Being a member of the committee of LAGIP — Lesbians And Gays In Probation (the NPS LGB&T support group) for 15 years including around 7 years as Vice Chair/ Chair then back to Vice Chair and a member of the original steering group for a:gender, a pan civil service trans network
- Serving on NPS/ NOMS diversity boards/ groups, Salford Police Independent Advisory Group, Greater Manchester Police Strategic IAG and GMPT LGB&T Focus Groups
- Practising as a volunteer counsellor specialising in gender variant clients and as a Counselling Supervisor — supervising other counsellors
- Being Chair of Inner Enigma, the Manchester based transsexual support charity.
- Involvement in around 10 trans support groups around the country and meeting in excess of 1,000 trans individuals.

Whilst I feel that this gives me a solid foundation upon which to base my hypotheses, it is important to note that no blind testing can be done to provide 'proof' to normally acceptable standards — and there may well be alternative approaches or ideas that fit the empirical evidence that I've observed over the last twenty plus years. All I can do is present my views, explain how I came to them and leave you to reach your own conclusions as to their value.

When I provide workshops on trans issues, I like to establish what delegates are expecting from my presentations — I then tell them that *my* expectations are to answer a few of their questions but make them think of a hundred others! I hope that this book achieves the same. I certainly don't have all of the answers and there will be some who question my views but if it gets readers thinking about the issues and implications of being trans then my objective will have been achieved.

My thanks go to individuals who spared the time to attend one of my presentations on trans issues and whose questions have helped to develop those talks and provide the basis for this book.

Helen Dale

Salford

February 2018 updated 2021 and 2023.

Chapter 2 Definitions

What does 'Transgender' mean?

The term 'transgender' is one of a number of labels used to describe individuals who do not fit conventional boundaries in terms of their gender identity. They may have physical characteristics of one sex but also have a very strong sense of being a different gender (or not having a gender at all). You may notice that I have switched from 'sex' to 'gender' in this explanation. This is quite deliberate, as it is the difference between the two that is significant when discussing trans.

The transgender 'spectrum' covers a wide range of 'conditions' that appear to have similar manifestations and may or may not be related.

A word of warning: put ten trans people in a room and I guarantee you'll come up with at least a dozen different definitions. There is no complete consensus — and interpretations do change. The following aims to provide a general view of terminology as used in 2023 — and to define how I use the labels in this book.

Transgender v Transexual

The term '**transgender**' is being used increasingly instead of '**transsexual**' rather than as an umbrella term. As there are occasions in this book where there is a distinction between those who may permanently transition from one perceived gender to another and others who do not, I use the term '**transsexual**' for the former and 'trans' as the umbrella term.

Trans and Intersex Labels:

Sex, Gender, Gender Identity & Gender Roles, Masculinity/ Femininity

For the purposes of this book, '**Sex**' relates to physical characteristics while '**Gender**'/ '**Gender Identity**' is concerned with who we are, how we feel. As gender is often seen these days to be synonymous with sex, referring to gender identity clarifies the meaning.

Gender Role is based on what is stereotypically expected of males and females in terms of the jobs they do and what is or is not appropriate for each sex. **Masculinity / Femininity** are based on stereotypical behaviours or feelings of individuals independent of their actual gender.

Assigning Sex

Doctors, midwives or nurses look at newborn infants and, based on what they see between the legs announce that it is a boy or girl. In the vast majority of cases, there is absolutely no problem with this pronouncement. For them, sex and gender are the same. But in a few cases, the individual's gender identity is different to their physical characteristics even though their genitalia may well be clearly defined as 'male' or 'female'. In other cases, the genitalia may be ambiguous. In that case, they may be **Intersex** (IS).

Transgender Spectrum

I have tended to refer to transition from one gender to another. This implies a binary structure of gender. This is overly simplistic and some individuals do not identify as male or female. Where I don't consider that it affects the validity of explanations and for simplicity, I will reflect a binary approach — covering non-binary where there are significantly different implications.

AFAB / AMAB

Assigned Female at Birth; Assigned Male at Birth — used rather than 'born female' or 'born male' as the latter implies that one's 'true' gender depends on physical characteristics rather than how we identify.

Affirmed Gender

One's gender after transitioning from that assigned at birth. Our innate gender.

Androgen Insensitivity Syndrome (AIS)

The individual has XY (male) chromosomes but the foetus is highly resistant to the effects of testosterone so visually is feminine — externally. The absence of the second X chromosome means that the individual does not develop female reproductive organs. This may only come to light when the individual fails to show signs of puberty. It is only then that investigation may reveal that the individual does not have female internal organs.

Acquired Gender

A term used in the Gender Recognition Act 2004 to refer to the gender in which a trans person lives and presents to the world.

Body Dysmorphia/ Body Map

The *'Phantom Limb'* syndrome is well reported — where individuals have lost limbs but feel that those limbs are still there; sometimes causing significant distress. Body Dysmorphia may be the reverse of this — where the brain's map of the body doesn't include a particular part.

It seems quite reasonable, for example, to expect the process that instigates the development, or not, of sexual organs during foetal growth to include the mapping of the relevant parts in the brain. If the brain remains significantly female despite the body developing as male, it may, for example, mean that the penis develops physically but is not present on the brain's map of the body — and the individual feels that it doesn't belong to them.

Whilst this may be reported in a significant proportion of trans individuals, it is not necessarily restricted to gender variant individuals. I had a client once who identified as a gay male with no desire to change genders — but wanted to have his penis removed as he didn't feel it belonged to him.

Chapter 2 Definitions

Cisgender
An individual born with matching sex and gender identity. I.e. not trans / gender variant.

Cisnormative
Presenting as a Cisgender person rather than as a trans person; trying to remain Stealth; the assumption that everyone is Cisgender.

Crossdresser (CD)
See Transvestite (TV)/ Crossdresser (CD)

Dead Name
The former / birth name of a trans person. Many trans people feel that they have no connection with this name after transition and don't want to be reminded of it. It may cause offence to ask a trans person what their original name was.

Drag Artists/ Female Impersonators
On stage/ in show business; drag artists are typically in pubs and clubs while female impersonators tend to imitate celebrities or styles.

Drag Queens (DQ)
Drag Queens parody rather than imitate women.

Drag Kings
Female equivalents of Drag Queens

Female Impersonators
See Drag Artists/ Female Impersonators

Gender Bender
Challenging conventions around gender presentation without fully presenting as the opposite gender. 2014 Eurovision Song Contest winner Conchita Wurst who dresses as a female but has full facial hair would probably fit into this category — or into drag queen/ artist. Some individuals in the Gay Village in Manchester wore short tartan skirts (definitely NOT kilts) — whilst dressing otherwise as male and with no attempt to present a female shape. Glam rock — with men wearing make-up — might also fit into this label.

Gender bending might be regarded as a personal expression similar to Goths rather than a transgender variation. One can argue, however, that choosing to mix gender stereotypes rather than others may indicate a degree of being transgender.

Gender Dysphoria
Gender Dysphoria has been the usual medical name for the condition where the individual's gender and sex do not match. This is often described as 'feeling you are in the wrong body'. Some individuals prefer **Gender Incongruence** (which is increasingly used) or **Gender Variance**. They suggest that *'Dysphoria'* indicates that the condition is an abnormality. *'Incongruence'* still suggests something 'wrong' — *'Gender Variance'* implies that differences are to be expected

Chapter 2 Definitions

Gender Fluid

Describes an individual whose gender identity varies over time. They may sometimes identify as male sometimes as female and sometimes as neither. The boundary between this and transvestism is likely to be blurred as both may switch between presentations. The two are not, however, the same.

Gender Incongruence

Previously referred to as '**Gender Dysphoria**', this is when the individual's innate Gender Identity is different to their physical sexual characteristics. This group probably covers the vast majority of individuals who identify as trans.

Gender Queer/ Gender Warriors

See Non-binary

Gender Variance

Gender Dysphoria has been the usual medical name for the condition where the individual's gender and sex do not match. This is often described as 'feeling you are in the wrong body'. Some individuals prefer Gender Incongruence (which is increasingly used) or 'Gender Variance'. 'Gender Dysphoria' indicates that the condition is an abnormality. 'Gender Incongruence' still suggests something 'wrong' — 'Gender Variance' implies that differences are to be expected as part of a wider range of options.

Intersex (IS)

Intersex covers a number of conditions where the individual has indeterminate or ambiguous sexual characteristics. This may or may not be apparent at birth. In the past, if the condition was apparent, they would often be 'assigned' to the sex of the most dominant genital characteristic very soon after birth. More recently, the decision has been deferred until later in life so that the individuals themselves can decide whether they identify as male or female (or neither).

Intersex is always congenital and can originate from genetic, chromosomal or hormonal variations or a combination of these. Environmental influences such as endocrine disruptors can also play a role in some intersex conditions.

Whilst intersex conditions may have different causes to transsexual conditions, if the individual is assigned to the 'wrong' sex at birth, they may well subsequently want similar treatment to transsexual individuals to transition to their true gender.

Most intersex people identify as male or female and feel no reason to alter their bodies. Others prefer not to be assigned to either male or female and identify as a 3rd sex — even to the extent of wanting to have both sets of genitalia.

Intersex people represent a significant percentage of the population with estimates ranging from 1.7% to 4% which means it is as common as someone being red-haired.

Inbetweenie/ Intergendered

See Non-binary

Lady Boys

See She-Males/ LadyBoys

Chapter 2 Definitions

Non-binary

Do not identify as 'male' or 'female' — or as both. Some individuals who prefer to identify as a gender that is neither male nor female may also use the term Gender Warriors, Transgender Warriors, Gender Queer, Transgendered, Pan-gendered, Inbetweenie, and Intergendered. Some self-descriptions from the Trans Mental Health Study 2012 (see bibliography) are given below.

'I do not feel like "man" is an accurate word to describe me. More accurate than "woman", but still not quite who I am. I often describe myself as a "boy", not really as an infantilism, but I think because it seems less rigidly defined. I also look more like a boy than a man since I am not taking hormones.'

[I have] a female identity that is strong, and a male identity that is usually weaker, sometimes they are in balance and sometimes male is stronger but I generally consider myself as gender non-conformist female, or androgyne or more recently fluid.

'A year ago, my gender identity was Not Woman. I now identify as male, but part of the reason for that is that it's easier than identifying as non-binary. If there were more accepted genders, I would probably be 'just masculine of centre'.'

Pan-gendered

See Non-binary

She-Males/ LadyBoys

Retain male genitalia and often have breast enhancements; may be (but are not necessarily) pre-op transsexual. The term 'She-Male' is usually ascribed to individuals offering 'exotic' sex due to a combination of breasts and penis. LadyBoy is used more to describe an entertainer (eg LadyBoys of Bangkok). These terms are often offensive to transsexual people.

Stealth

Living as a non-trans person — blending into the general community. Concealing a trans history.

Supertranny

Highly glamorous rather than over the top; often have breast enhancements and often work in show business.

Trannie/ Tranny

Slang for TVs (and cross-dressers) Many trans individuals, especially transsexual individuals, are often offended if referred to as a tranny. Like the term 'Queer' and the racist 'N-word' it has been reclaimed by parts of the community and adopted as a badge of pride.

Trans/ Trans*

Abbreviation which tends to cover individuals who are living and presenting in role full time rather than those who switch between roles — so includes transgender in the sense of not wanting to have surgery and transsexual. Trans issues in this sense may also include intersexed individuals who were 'wrongly' assigned at birth. The use of trans* with the asterisk at the end uses the computing convention where the * can be anything after the root — so can include transgender, transvestite, transsexual etc.

Transgender (TG)

The term transgender used to be used either as an umbrella term to cover the entire spectrum of atypical gender identity — or, more specifically, to describe individuals who spend most or even all of their lives living in an 'acquired' gender role — but have no wish to undergo gender reassignment surgery. It is, however, increasingly being used as an alternative to and synonymous with 'transsexual'.

Transgender Warriors

See Non-binary

Transsexual (TS)

Whilst TVs/ CDs/ DQs and others switch between perceived gender roles, transsexual individuals do not. They need to polarise and transition, if possible. Sometimes medical reasons may preclude treatment. The term transsexual should be used as an adjective or adverb but not as a noun. So, you may refer to someone as a transsexual individual or say he/she is or they are transsexual — but not, for example, she is a transsexual.

Transsexual describes one aspect of me — it does not define me.

Transsexual individuals fall within the 2010 Equality Act definition for those with the protected characteristic of 'Gender Reassignment': 'proposing to undergo, is undergoing or has undergone Gender Reassignment'.

Transman

A female-to-male transsexual individual

Transvestite (TV)/ Crossdresser (CD)

Basically the same — but the terms can have different implications depending on where you are or who you talk to.

In the UK, some consider the term 'transvestite' attempts to put a medical label on them and they prefer the term 'Cross-dresser'; others feel that the term CD is more appropriate for someone who may wear women's underwear but have no desire to present a full female image. In the USA, the term TV also implies cross-dressers who have sex with men. In the UK we tend to separate the concepts of sexual orientation from gender identity and would refer to a gay or bi-transvestite or cross-dresser.

Basically, however, the term transvestite is simply Latin for cross-dressing.

Usually, men who dress as women but there are also female transvestites who dress as men — including flattening their breasts, putting a filled sock in the front of their trousers and even wearing false beards or moustaches.

Transvestites do not normally have any desire to change roles permanently or undergo gender reassignment surgery. A few do take hormones or have breast implants to create a more feminine figure. One suggested way of looking at TVs is to think of them as day trippers from one gender to another (while transsexual individuals permanently emigrate and gender fluid are on a permanent voyage of exploration).

Chapter 2 Definitions

Dictionary definitions of transvestism often describe it as being 'for purposes of sexual gratification'. Whilst transvestites do often describe themselves as 'feeling sexy' when dressed, it is more common for them to report feeling 'relaxed' or 'just **right**'. It is certainly misleading to assume that because transvestites often feel sexy when dressed that sexual gratification is the driving force.

Transwoman
A male-to-female transsexual individual

Other Related Terms

Forms of address
In dealing with trans individuals, their preferences should be observed with respect to forms of address or reference. Transsexual individuals living in role will usually prefer to be addressed appropriately to the role in which they live. Transvestites may prefer to be addressed in a manner appropriate to how they are dressed at the time. In formal situations (perhaps if being questioned at a police station or treated at a hospital) transvestites may appreciate an opportunity to get changed.

Gender neutral forms of address
Individuals identifying as Non-binary prefer alternatives to 'He', 'She' 'His' 'Hers'. Some may accept 'They' / 'Their'; others prefer:

Traditional pronouns	He/ She/ They	His/ Her/ Their	Him/ Her/ Them
Non-binary pronouns	E, Ey, Hu, Jee, Peh, Per, Thon, Shi, Ve, Xe, Ze, Zhe	Eir, S, Hir, Hus, Jeir, Peh's, Per, Thons, Vis, Xyr, Zer, Zes, Zher(s), Zir	Em, 'H, Hum, Jem, Mer, Pehm, Per, Thon, Ver, Xem, Zhim

There will almost certainly be new alternatives added to the list while others fall into disuse. In my experience, it is only individuals who identify as non-binary who prefer the alternative pronouns.

GRS
Historically taken to stand for Gender Reassignment Surgery — but many trans people will say that their gender has not been changed and they prefer to consider that it stands for genital reconstruction surgery. Often referred to as a 'sex change'.

LGBT
Lesbian, Gay, Bisexual, Transgender (may also include A- Asexual or Ally, I-Intersex, Q-Queer and other initials),

Neo-vagina
The vagina constructed during GRS.

Passing
Not being identified as trans when in public

Chapter 2 Definitions

Pre-op/ Post-op
Before/ after gender reassignment surgery.

Sexual Orientation
Who an individual is attracted to sexually. May be:

Heterosexual — attracted to the opposite sex;

Homosexual/ Gay/ Lesbian — attracted to the same sex

Bisexual — attracted to either/ both sexes (reflects binary genders)

Pan-sexual — attracted to more than one sex (without binary limits)

A-sexual — is not sexually attracted to others. Within the 'A-sexual' grouping, 16 subgroups have been identified including *Graysexual* — experiences attraction infrequently or experiences it but doesn't wish to pursue any relationship with the person, *Demisexual* — might experience sexual attraction toward someone after an emotional bond is formed.

Many trans individuals feel uncomfortable having sexual relations pre-op because they have the wrong genitalia and do not want to have a partner who is attracted to them because they are 'exotic'.

Polyamorous — open to non-monogamous relationships

Whilst there may well be a link between the root cause of Gender Identity and Sexual Orientation — the two are independent of each other. There is, however, evidence that the structures of male homosexual brains are more like that of heterosexual females and those of lesbians are more like male brains.

Trans individuals may be of any sexual orientation.

Social Transition
See Transition

Stealth
Living in an acquired gender role without revealing a trans history

Transition
The permanent full-time adoption of the gender role with which the individual identifies. Usually starts with social transition where the individual presents in the gender role with which they identify before any medical treatment such as hormones. The transition process continues until the individual has made all of the changes they feel are appropriate to their individual situation. This may or may not include medical interventions such as hormone treatment and surgery.

Other Abbreviations used in this Guide

GMPT — Greater Manchester Probation Trust

NOMS — National Offender Management Service (combined Prison and Probation Services) (Now known as HMPPS His Majesty's Prison and Probation Service).

Chapter 3 Causality

Gender Variations

If asked to define what makes a man or woman, or how they are different, most people will refer to sex organs, breasts, chromosomes, physical attributes such as height and build — or to the presence or absence of body hair or an Adam's apple or baldness. Certainly, all of these factors are, typically, different between male and female.

The evidence shows that there are other innate characteristics — our gender identity, sexual orientation and body map[1].

Gender identity is the key as far as this book is concerned — but the other factors demonstrate the variations that are present in all humans.

In trans individuals, the mental characteristics are typically the opposite to those usually associated with the physical body — so you might have a female body map — despite 'male' chromosomes, sex organs, typical height and build.

I've included sexual orientation on the illustration because this can vary as well and whilst the two are different, there may be a link in causality.

Nurture v Nature

There is no universally accepted explanation of why these variations occur but I believe that the following is now acknowledged as the *probable* cause. The condition

---

[1] See Chapter 2 Definitions: Body Dysmorphia/Body Map

occurs when an individual has the physical characteristics of one sex and the psychological characteristics of the other, the 'female brain in a male body syndrome' (or vice versa). In fact, there is a total spectrum ranging from ultra-macho to extreme femininity with individuals at all points along this spectrum, regardless of their physical sex.

You only have to look around you to see that this is the case. As well as feminine women and macho men, we can all identify feminine males and masculine females. Trans is, I believe, an extreme version of this latter condition. In most cases, just like a see-saw, there is a tendency for the effect to come down on one side or the other.

In their book 'Brainsex[2]', Anne Moir and David Jessel go into considerable detail regarding the development of male and female brain patterns and support their findings with evidence from clinical trials. Whilst it does not go into any significant detail concerning trans (it concentrates on the difference between male and female brain structures and the effects of these differences), it does also explain how male bodies can have significantly female minds (and vice versa) — and how this 'opposite sex' element can vary in extent.

It has also been shown that the way males and females use different quadrants of the brain when processing information and the size of the hypothalamus are different. Again, the hypothalamus in transwomen (male-to-female) is that of a non-trans woman rather than that of a male (even before taking hormones).

What is the difference between Male and Female Brains?

Men and women are clearly different — not only in physical characteristics but mentally. Evolution has, over the millennia, produced bodies and minds which are adapted to the different traditional roles that men and women have adopted. The physical differences are usually obvious — but differences in mental approaches are also evident. Men tend to be more competitive, more aggressive, and more focused when dealing with problems. Women tend to consider far wider issues when making decisions — they've needed to become capable of multi-tasking to a greater extent: looking after children and preparing food etc.

This is self-evident. You only have to think about men and women that you know. There are, of course, women with masculine characteristics just as there are men with female characteristics. This isn't stereotyping — it's just the way natural selection has worked.

Various questionnaires demonstrate the different mental approaches — including ones that focus on the different parts of

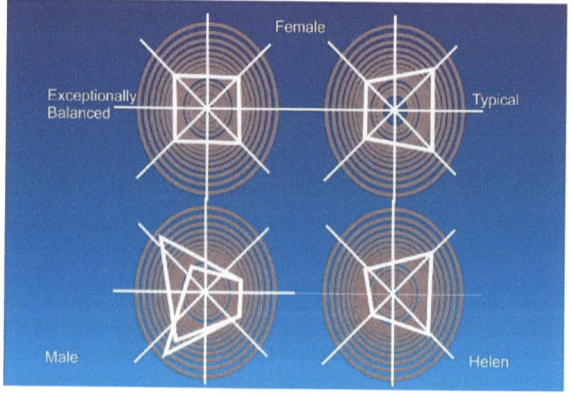

---

[2] See bibliography

the brain are used. Women tend to use the four quadrants approximately equally — perhaps with slightly more use of the right quadrants — while men have a very clear emphasis on one of the two left hand quadrants. As you can see, my own mapping is much more typical of a female profile.

Other tests also demonstrate the difference in men's and women's typical responses to questions. Given multiple choices for 30 questions and scoring 'A' answers as 15; 'B's as 5 and 'C's as minus 5; scores can be plotted on a chart.

I have often used these live at presentations — then plotted the results. In almost every case the 'male' scores have been at the bottom and 'female' scores at the top. A small number of male-to-female trans scores sit consistently in the female range. There is an overlap area but the different ranges are clear.

Occasionally there have been 'rogue' scores apparently in the 'wrong' ranges; but every time this has occurred the individual has identified as LGB or T. While these 'brain tests' are far from diagnostic tools to assess whether someone is or is not trans, they do demonstrate a difference between the genders.

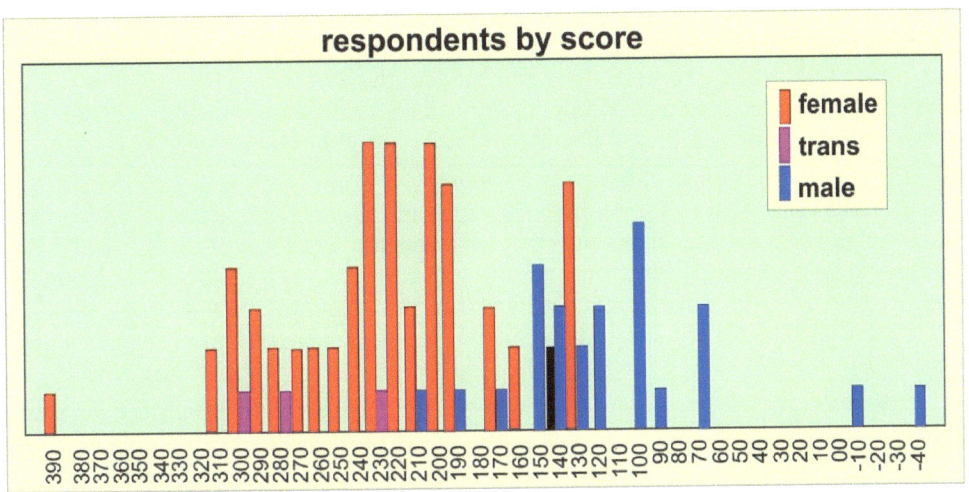

So what happens to define Brain Sex?

It has long been understood that genes are responsible for our physical and mental characteristics.

Pairs of chromosomes — 22 each from the mother and father — control eye colour, the size and shape of features such as the nose etc. One final pair of chromosomes (theoretically) determines whether the foetus develops as male or female. The mother provides an X chromosome; the father can provide either an X or a Y chromosome. If the combination is XX then the baby *should* be female; if it's XY, it *should* develop as male. (There are other rarer possible combinations, which can also affect the development – see section on Intersex).

But this is not the whole story. All foetuses initially have the capacity to develop as either male or female and this development depends on the presence or absence of male hormones. If male hormones are present, the baby will appear male even if its chromosomes are XX. If they are absent, the baby will appear to be female even if the chromosomes are XY.

At about 6 weeks, an XY foetus develops special cells, which produce male hormones. The presence of these hormones programmes the body to develop as male — and not to develop the female sex organs.

The default state of the embryonic brain at this stage is female. Male hormones produced by the foetus start to reprogramme the brain structure from female to male. The burst of male hormones at this time is at a level which is 4 times that which will be present during early childhood and is only achieved again at puberty. If the male hormones are absent, the brain retains its original female structure. All males, therefore, have gone through a 'sex change' during pregnancy!

This brain 'reprogramming' takes time to complete.

It is now known that male foetuses can generate sufficient hormones to trigger the development of male sex organs — but not at a sufficient level to completely reprogramme the brain.

Clinical experiments (using animals) demonstrate that different levels of male hormones at this critical stage can make the brain more or less male. This applied to both differing strengths of hormones and the length of time to which the brain was exposed to the hormones. Whilst clinical trials have not been undertaken on humans (they would be unethical), it is believed that the same applies to humans.

Clearly a variation in the extent to which the brain was reprogrammed and a consequential variation in the relative strengths of the male and female sides to that brain explains why there is such a spectrum of masculinity/ femininity. It is self-evident that very few brains are 100% converted — or, in the case of females, left completely unaltered. Very few men are totally macho without any feminine traits at all — and very few women display totally feminine behaviour in every respect. Nearly everyone has some 'opposite sex' brain structure. In the case of men, this is probably just as well.

The trans individual is simply at one end of the spectrum which ranges from virtually no 'opposite sex' brain pattern to one which is virtually completely that expected for the opposite sex.

Genetic Influences

Genetic influences are not the only, or even the primary, cause of being trans.

There is, however, evidence of a genetic factor that influences the susceptibility of the foetus to the effects of testosterone. This would explain the clustering of cases within families which occurs; whilst variations in the strength and duration of the flow of testosterone may override any genetic factor and result in exceptional cases. A genetically low susceptibility to the effects of testosterone would require a greater strength/duration of the flow to produce a 'normal' effect, whereas a high susceptibility may only need a relatively weak or short flow to achieve the same effect.

This clustering also shows a higher-than-average incidence of gay family members — which suggests to me that sexual orientation is also affected by the flow of testosterone. If the 'default' (female) state is an attraction to men and this is unchanged whilst the body is changed, it would naturally result in same-sex attraction. There are

Chapter 3 Causality

also other genetic conditions that appear to be more common amongst trans individuals.

Social Conditioning

A case in the USA involving a young boy whose penis had been destroyed during circumcision has been cited in the past as demonstrating that it is possible to condition an individual into a gender role. This case was the subject of television documentaries and a book[3]

According to these sources, the doctor convinced the parents that the child would be happier as a girl — and they agreed to genital reconstruction surgery and to bring up the child as a girl. The doctor later announced that he had followed up the case and that the child had adapted successfully to her new role. It was some years later that the truth emerged and it was learnt that the boy had never been happy as a girl and that he had reverted to male role[4]. Instead of proving that it was possible to condition someone into an acquired gender role, it proved the exact reverse — that despite conditioning, an individual's gender shows through.

My own history, and that of other individuals I know, supports that argument. I grew up in an RAF family, I was a keen member of the scouting movement — joining the Wolf Cubs as soon as I was able and graduating through Boy Scouts, Senior Scouts and Rovers (as they then were), I also joined the Army Cadets at school (it didn't have Air Training Corps) and wanted to be a pilot in the RAF. I later joined the Territorial Army. Hardly a stereotypical 'feminine upbringing' and, if conditioning was to be effective, I would have been a 'man's man'! Yet throughout this, I was also cross-dressing whenever possible. Even now, post-transition, I enjoy adventurous activities that have traditionally been seen as masculine.

I believe that social conditioning DOES affect being trans — but in a negative rather than a positive manner.

Social conditioning tells trans individuals that it is wrong for a man to dress as a female — and this leads to guilt, shame and secrecy. We tend to be reluctant to let others know of our being trans for fear of ridicule and rejection. Whenever things went seriously wrong in my life, I saw it as punishment from God for my evil behaviour and the first thing I would do was to get rid of my female items!

Most trans individuals hide their 'dressing' and try to 'give it up'. In trying to suppress being trans we experience considerable stress.

Many never come to terms with it. Some, faced with ultimatums from partners to 'give it up or else' or pressure from families, colleagues or the wider community, commit suicide.

This social conditioning acts as a 'brake' on our being trans. It is reinforced at stages during our lives when other major events occur. This explains why so many trans individuals experience periods of 'purging' — especially when involved in new relationships, getting married, having children etc. Career challenges may suppress the TG drive.

---

[3] See bibliography: As Nature Made Him

[4] Sadly, the individual concerned committed suicide in 2004.

Chapter 3 Causality

Gradually, however, many aspects of this conditioning tend to diminish — as does our concentration on those aspects which may have helped to suppress the drive.

This allows the drive to emerge (or, more likely, to re-emerge).

In many cases, significant events — such as the breakdown of a marriage or the death of a partner — result in a substantial reduction in the braking forces. The trans drive suddenly emerges very strongly.

Transgender Continuum

I used to hold the view that transvestism and transsexuality had different causes. There were, obviously, similarities between the two conditions but transvestites did not 'become' transsexuals.

I have, however, met a significant number of trans individuals who, like myself, started by considering themselves to be transvestite — then later deciding that they were transsexual. There is an argument that we were always transsexual but did not realise or accept it.

It is now apparent that there is a continuous spectrum from almost 100% female brain to almost 100% male brain — with people at every stage along that scale and that this can occur regardless of whether the body has male or female genitalia. In the case of a 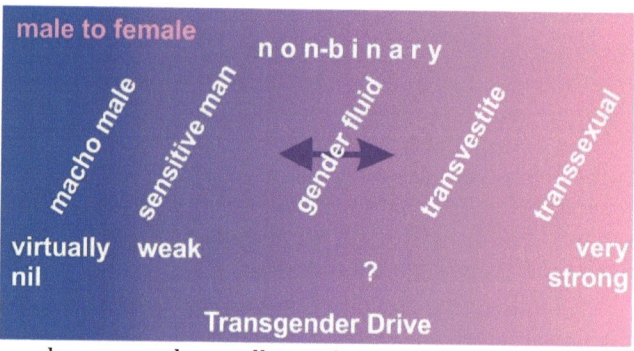 male body, at one end of the scale you get the totally macho male — at the other the ultra-feminine transsexual who never accepted that her body matched her mind.

Between these two extremes, will be men who are happy to be men but have some feminine characteristics, further along the scale will be potential transvestites, gender fluid and non-binary individuals; further still they will be potentially transsexual. Similarly, those assigned female at birth may range from ultra-femme to transsexual. Whilst there are female transvestites most of the individuals who transition from female to male, in my experience, tend to have identified as lesbian or gay.

TG Drive v Braking Force

I call the force that results from this 'opposite gender influence' the 'TG drive'. The higher the female to male brain ratio — the stronger the TG drive that will be experienced by the individual. I see this force as the 'lift' in a hot air balloon.

I say 'potential' transvestites and transsexual because the TG drive may be suppressed for years by braking forces.

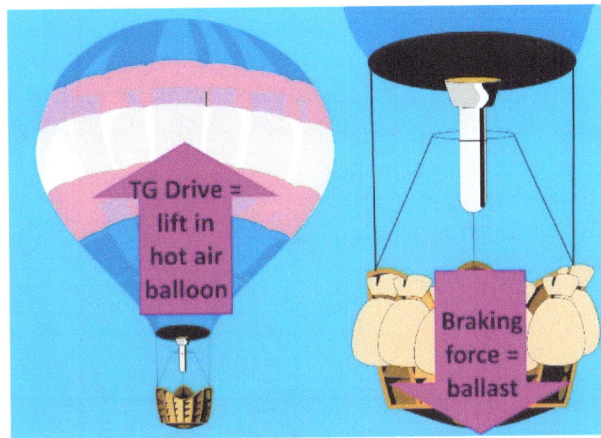

Those braking forces are, I believe, where social conditioning comes into the equation. They are like the hot air balloon's ballast and include:

- Society's expectations — that 'men should be men'
- Religious beliefs
- Focus on other events
- Lack of awareness of possible treatment
- Responsibilities — especially families
- And I'm sure hormone levels play their part.

Just as the innate 'drive' can vary, so too can the braking forces. There may be a powerful drive restrained by huge braking forces — or a smaller drive held back by smaller braking forces.

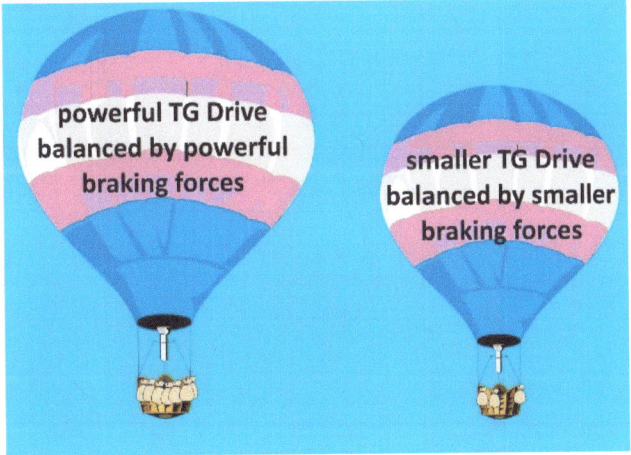

Those braking forces will tend to diminish.

- We start to question and challenge our conditioning
- Our focus on other issues diminishes
- Responsibilities may be reduced
- Relationships may get into a rut
- Testosterone levels reduce as we get older
- And, as we become aware of possible options, the braking forces are removed and the TG drive is released

Chapter 3 Causality

Like a pressure cooker, you can try to suppress the drive but, if you do, the pressure will build and ultimately explode. For transvestites, it may be that cross-dressing acts as a safety valve.

Chapter 4 Social Transition

For many trans individuals, surgery is seen as the most important step in their transition but, in reality, social transition is the biggest change they will make. This is when they stop presenting in the gender they were assigned at birth and become their 'Affirmed Gender'.

This step may be taken overnight — but is much more likely to be spread over several months or even longer.

Whilst a significant number of male-to-female individuals may always have identified as transsexual often described as 'being in the wrong body' many older transwomen (perhaps two-thirds) have spent years identifying as transvestite before accepting that they are transsexual. There wasn't the awareness of transgender issues when they were younger and there certainly wasn't the legal protection and increasing acceptance of the subject.

They may have been married and have children – all of whom may be affected by their decision to transition.

Just as many older transwomen have previously identified as transvestite, a very significant number, possibly the majority, of transmen have previously identified as lesbian or gay women.

Younger trans individuals are now able to find out about the subject through an array of media coverage; some bad, some indifferent and, occasionally, some positive. They have access to the internet – unheard of just twenty years ago – where they can find support and advice. Many of them, including young children, are now able to realise that they are not alone in feeling as they do; that there is a solution and they can avoid some of the issues that the older generation faced.

This isn't to suggest that the process is easy now. It's not. There are still many individuals who oppose trans rights and their right to exist.

Social transition may include changing names, the way in which they present, single-sex facilities they expect to use and a large number of official and other records.

Deciding to Transition

Just reaching the decision that transition is appropriate for an individual can often take years.

It might start with a suspicion that they are transsexual rather than transvestite – but the braking forces described in the previous chapter (especially fear of the consequences of that decision) may discourage them from taking any steps towards transition.

This suspicion may grow into an acceptance that they are transsexual – but they are still reluctant to do anything about it. Eventually, they may conclude that continuing as they are is no longer an option and, despite reservations, they need to make changes.

Even at this stage, other considerations may prevent them from doing anything immediately. If they have families, they may wait until children are old enough to understand – or until they have finished their education. In some cases, the need to work may mean they defer transition until they retire. Whilst the law prohibits discrimination (see below), many trans people do lose their jobs as a consequence of transition.

Legal Protection

As soon as someone 'intends to undergo' 'gender reassignment', they fall within the 'Protected Characteristic' of 'Gender Reassignment' as defined by the Equality Act 2010 and are protected against discrimination. They need not be having any medical treatment to come under that definition.

Changing Names (different rules apply in Scotland)

Individuals can change their names legally whether or not transitioning and it is not necessary to follow any legal process unless you need documentation to apply for or change official documents. This is usually done by either a Deed Poll or a Statutory Declaration.

Deed Poll

You can make your own Deed Poll using wording that is published on the www.gov.uk website but some organisations may require that the Deed Poll be 'enrolled' with the Royal Courts of Justice and this is not possible with a Deed Poll you have made yourself. There is a fee for enrolling the Deed Poll.

Statutory Declaration

A Statutory Declaration is similar to a Deed Poll except that it is signed in the presence of a solicitor, notary public, justice of the peace, commissioner for oaths or another qualified person. It does not need to be enrolled.

Changing Names in Scotland

Details of the process for changing names in Scotland are available on the National Records of Scotland website www.nrscotland.gov.uk. The individual's birth needs to have been registered in Scotland, or there must be an entry in the Adopted Children Register, Parental Order Register or the Gender Recognition Register.

The applicant can download the required forms, complete and submit them to National Records of Scotland. The forms do not need to be completed by a solicitor etc nor do they need to be witnessed.

Impact of Transition on Relationships

If a trans person has a partner; their transition may impact on the perceived nature of their relationship. If the couple have been in a heterosexual relationship, then it may now be seen by the outside world as gay. If it has been a gay relationship, it may now be seen as heterosexual. In either case, it can create the impression that the partner has now changed their sexual orientation. A woman whose partner is M to F may be considered by her friends, family and acquaintances as lesbian; whilst a gay man whose partner is going through the same process may now be seen as 'straight'. Similarly, if the individual is F to M the partner may now be judged to be gay if a male or straight if female. Yet the partner's sexual orientation hasn't necessarily changed.

This may be particularly problematic if the partner's beliefs are against same-sex relationships/ homosexuality.

There are cases of individuals being prepared to accept a partner transitioning and stay with them but not to allow the marriage to become legally one between two individuals of the same sex. This may prevent the transitioning individual from seeking legal recognition in their acquired gender.

Gender Stereotypes

The NHS Gender Identity Clinics had a reputation for expecting patients, especially transwomen, to fit into gender stereotypes: wearing skirts or dresses and high heels (not jeans, T-shirts and Doc Martens), full make-up, feminine hairstyles etc. Failure to do so was reputed to delay their progress.

In the real world, of course, women dress as they wish to suit their own personalities which are infinitely variable and there should be no pressure on trans people to follow any stereotypes if they don't wish to do so.

However, notwithstanding the previous paragraph, when transitioning with people who have known the individual for many years in the gender they were assigned at birth, it is common for them to forget to use appropriate names and gender pronouns. They may also struggle to understand why the individual is transitioning if they have not previously portrayed traits associated with their acquired gender. At that stage, it can be useful to reinforce the change message by adopting some stereotypes. This can be a balance between achieving a desired outcome (not being misgendered) and behaving in an exaggerated way for a time.

Many trans people, especially transwomen, going through transition also tend to give up what have been perceived as 'masculine' interests such as football, motor racing, adventure sports etc. when, in reality, many women DO enjoy such activities as well.

Avoiding Attention in Public

The Trans Mental Health Study 2012[5] showed that the number of trans people who have experienced the following are:

Silent harassment (being stared at/ whispered about for being trans)	81%
Been made fun off or called names	73%
Experienced sexual harassment (eg cat calling, being propositioned)	38%
Been hit or beaten up	19%
Been sexually assaulted	14%
Been raped	6%

Trans people, especially transwomen, may, therefore, want to avoid attracting attention in public by blending into the local environment. This may be particularly important in the early stages of transition when confidence may be fragile.

---

[5] See bibliography

Presentations that blend in for shopping in Harrods or Harvey Nichols in Knightsbridge are likely to stand out in Lidl or Aldi in a depressed city centre.

As a trans person gains confidence they may well be able to cope better with attracting attention and dealing with or ignoring the consequential misgendering and abuse.

Ideally, of course, there shouldn't be any abuse and it should not be necessary for trans people to make the adjustments. While the situation is much better than it was even twenty years ago, if racism, sexism and homophobia are anything to go by, this isn't likely to be the case for decades. In the meantime, it is sensible to take care to avoid problems.

Non-Binary / Gender Fluid Social Transition

Defining 'social transition' for most binary identifying individuals is relatively straightforward; those assigned male at birth present as female and those assigned female at birth present as male. For 'non-binary' or 'gender fluid' individuals it is not a linear process with a fixed start (gender assigned at birth) and an end point where the individual's body aligns with their gender identity. As their gender identity may not be a fixed point on the gender continuum their presentation may be androgynous or a mixture of stereotypical gender presentations.

Some non-binary individuals describe their journey as an unending 'blossoming'. Intersex individuals who also identify as non-binary may be 'becoming more aware of their biological realities and making decisions based on their biological; sex- identity and gender identity[6]'.

---

[6] Sara Kelly in What It Means to Transition When You're Non-Binary, TeenVogue, https://www.teenvogue.com/story/non-binary-transitioning, Joshua M Ferguson 30 Nov 2017

Chapter 5 Myth Busting

The media have sensationalised reports about trans individuals and created numerous myths about the community. Some of the following myths are mentioned elsewhere in this book but I make no apology for summarising them here.

Myth No 1: Sex = Gender

Biological sex is related to physical characteristics. Gender is how we identify and who we really are. In spiritual terms, it might be compared to the body and the soul. In most cases, sex and gender are aligned. For trans people, this may not be the case.

Myth No 2: Sex is Binary

'There are only two sexes: male and female and everyone is simply one or the other. Only humans are sufficiently misguided to think that we can change'.

Gynandromorphic examples (displaying characteristics of both sexes) have been found in many species including butterflies, lobsters, crabs, spiders, ticks, flies, locusts, crickets, dragonflies, ants, termites, bees, lizards, snakes, rodents, and many species of birds. The Cardinal (right) is male on one side and female on the other.

Myth No 3: Chromosomes XX = Female, XY= Male

This simplistic assumption is good enough for most discussions. Knowledge has, however, developed in this field as it has in other areas.

At the end of the 19th century, it was found humans had 46 chromosomes and that all males in a group had XY chromosomes and all the women in that group had XX. The conclusion was that the Y chromosome defined 'male'.

Then, in the 1940s it was found that some men had 47 chromosomes including XXY – whilst some women had 45 with only a single X.

When DNA was discovered, it was found that there was an SrY gene – usually on the Y chromosome. Sometimes, however, it was missing and, in other cases, it was on another chromosome. The result was that there were 46XX men and 46XY women and some men didn't have the SrY gene but some women did.

So, it was much more complex than XY=male and XX=female.

There were other complications. Androgen Insensitivity Syndrome prevented the flow of testosterone from triggering the development of male sex organs – leading to individuals who appear externally as female but have 46XY chromosomes. A situation that is sometimes only discovered when the individual is unable to conceive. (see also under Definitions).

Congenital Adrenal Hyperplasia masculinises 46XX individuals. Other syndromes such as 5 Alpha-reductase-2 deficiency can cause some babies to appear as one sex at birth and the other at puberty.

Overall, these intersex conditions are as common as being left-handed or having red hair.

Myth No 4: Sex Can't Change

The Clown Fish lives in colonies with just one female. When the female dies, one of the males changes sex to female.

Myth No 5: Transvestism is a fetish

Cross-dressing isn't fundamentally about sexual gratification. Some cross-dressers will say they 'feel sexy' when dressed and some do masturbate while dressed. The majority, however, describe 'feeling right' when dressed.

Some crossdressers may aim for an appearance that they consider 'sexy'. Most, in my experience, however, aim for a 'woman next door' look.

Myth No 6: All Transgender People have Surgery

Not all trans people want to have surgery. According to the European Union Agency for Fundamental Rights, 35% of transgender individuals in the UK had undergone surgery to 'change their body in a way that better matches their gender identity', 65% had not.

Myth No 7: Trans = Gay

Sexual orientation and gender identity are not the same.

Trans people can be sexually attracted to:
- Another gender
- The same gender
- More than one gender
- Regardless of gender
- Or experience no sexual attraction.

Myth No 8: Trans Women are a Threat

During the review of the Gender Recognition Act and the suggestion that the process should be by self-declaration, it was suggested that men would take advantage of 'legal recognition', self-declare as women and be able to access female spaces to attack women. It was then implied that trans women, themselves, were also a danger to other women.

I'm not clear how claiming to be transgender, therefore entitled to be in female spaces (with or without legal recognition of their gender), would diminish any attack they might carry out.

It seems laughable to me to suggest that a male, intent on attacking a woman in, say, a female toilet, would dress as a woman – and probably draw attention to themselves in the process. Surely it would be easier to pretend to be a cleaner with a mop and bucket.

Young People

Myth No 9: It's a Fad/ They are Attention Seeking

The large increase in young people claiming to be transgender has led to suggestions that it has become a fad or that the individuals are seeking attention. The reality is that increased awareness and an apparent increase in acceptance of LGBT identities has enabled young people to be more open about their feelings. There MAY be some individuals who 'jump on the bandwagon' but even if this is the case in a few instances, supporting them isn't likely to cause long term problems. Where it does prove to be a fad, the individual will probably move on to the next fashion trend.

Rejecting a young person's feelings is much more likely to cause problems.

Myth No 10: They are Too Young to Know

I have worked with young children who knew from a very early age that they were transgender – even if they didn't have the vocabulary to express it. They know what they are in the same way that they know they are right or left-handed.

Myth No 11: Exposed to Irreversible Changes

The sensationalist media imply that young children are exposed to irreversible changes including hormone treatment and surgery before they are old enough to know their own minds.

Young children are not given any treatment until they have demonstrated a consistent and deep routed cross-gender identity. Even then, they would not be prescribed hormone treatment until they are 16 or given surgery before they are 18.

They MAY be prescribed puberty blockers at an earlier age. These have routinely been prescribed for precocious puberty in cis-gender children. The biggest concern with puberty blockers is a possible loss of bone density – which can be countered with vitamin D and calcium. The alternative is to allow them to go through puberty and, in the case of trans girls, develop masculine features including fascial and body hair, Adams Apple and a deep voice – all of which will cause distress later. For trans boys, it would include breasts and necessitate mastectomies (and hysterectomies) later.

Chapter 6 Transsexual Journey to Surgery

WPATH Standards of Care

Medical support for transition should follow the World Professional Association for Transgender Health (WPATH) Standards of Care. These include guidelines on requirements for support, prescribing hormones and referrals for surgery.

NHS Gender Identity Clinics or Private

Trans individuals can (theoretically) choose between treatment on the NHS or from private providers. In practice, funding issues may preclude the private route – and very long waiting lists may force others to use private services.

Adults

England

At the time of writing (October 2023), there are seven NHS Gender Identity Clinics within England dealing with adults:

Exeter	Devon Partnership NHS Trust West of England Specialist Gender Identity Clinic
Daventry	Northamptonshire Healthcare NHS Foundation Trust Gender Identity Clinic
Leeds	Leeds and York Partnership NHS Foundation Trust Gender Identity Clinic
London	Tavistock and Portman NHS Foundation Trust Gender Identity Clinic for Adults
Newcastle	Northumberland, Tyne and Wear NHS Foundation Trust Northern Region Gender Dysphoria Service
Nottingham	Nottinghamshire Healthcare NHS Foundation Trust Centre for Transgender Health
Sheffield	Sheffield Health and Social Care NHS Foundation Trust Gender Identity Clinic

There are also four community-based services in England:

East of England	East of England Gender Service Cambridge another centre is planned for Norfolk
London	TransPlus
Manchester	Indigo Gender Clinic
Merseyside	CMAGIC

Northern Ireland:

| Belfast | Brackenburn Clinic Gender Identity Service |

Scotland:

Aberdeen	Grampian Gender Identity Clinic
Edinburgh	The Edinburgh Chalmers Gender Identity Clinic
Glasgow	Sandyford NHS Gender Identity Clinic
Inverness	Highland Gender Identity Service

Wales

| Cardiff | Gender Identity Wales |

Young People

In theory, there are two NHS centres for young people:

England and Wales	Gender Identity Development Service (GIDS) London and Leeds and outreach clinics. Not currently taking referrals
Scotland	Sandyford NHS Gender Identity Clinic

Private Providers

There are a number of private providers, including online services. They offer a far quicker pathway but at a significant price.

Referrals

Individuals generally need to be referred to the clinic by their GP although some GICs will accept self-referral. Once referred, there may be a significant delay before an appointment is offered. Private patients may self-refer to the psychiatrist.

Initial Appointments/ Diagnosis

Going through the GICs means much of the basic treatment is free — but is subject to the increasing demands on NHS and the consequential waiting lists, a degree of (perceived) 'gate-keeping' and bureaucratic delays at times. Private treatment can cut through some of the red tape — but can be costly. In either case, initial appointments should be followed by supervision visits typically every three months. (This frequency is not currently achieved by most of the GICs).

Real Life Experience (Real Life Test)

Whether the individual goes through the NHS or Private routes, they will be required to live in role for a period before being referred for surgery. This is the 'Real Life Experience' or 'Real Life Test'. The minimum period is a year but more typically two years with GICs.

Hormone Treatment

Male-to-Female
Male-to-female trans people will typically be prescribed oestrogen, usually as tablets, gel or patches. This may be supplemented by androgen/ testosterone blockers and/or progesterone.

Female-to-Male
Female-to-male trans individuals will typically be prescribed testosterone via injections or initially in the form of a gel.

The NHS may impose a waiting period before prescribing hormone treatment — up to a year in some cases while private practitioners may prescribe them on the second appointment, typically three months after the initial assessment. It has even been known for private practitioners to prescribe hormones on the first visit.

Electrolysis
Most transwomen planning to transition permanently (and others who want to avoid '5 o'clock shadow' showing through make-up) undergo electrolysis — usually needle or laser on the face and neck. Those who are undergoing GRS may also clear the genitals to avoid hair growing within the neo-vagina. Limited electrolysis is sometimes, but not always, funded by GICs.

Electrolysis (needle or laser) to remove facial hair may take two to three years to complete and cost £2-5,000. (2018 prices)

Speech Therapy
Transwomen who have been through male puberty will typically have a deeper voice than cis-females. They may be offered speech therapy to train their voice to sound more feminine. Trans-guy' voices usually 'break' as a result of the testosterone treatment.

Referral for surgery
Individuals who have completed their 'Real Life Experience' and have been assessed by two psychiatrists as ready may be referred for surgery. Not all trans individuals want surgery and medical reasons may prevent such procedures.

Male-to-female Surgical Procedures

GRS
The main surgery required by most transwomen is GRS, Gender Reassignment Surgery (also known by other names including Sex Reassignment Surgery and Gender Confirmation Surgery).

This entails a number of steps to create the neo-vagina from the penis (sometimes supplemented by other donor material); creating a cavity for the neo-vagina; relocating the urethra and using nerves from the tip of the penis to create a clitoris or g-spot. Other skin from the scrotum is used to create labia.

In some cases, the individual may opt for cosmetic or 'zero-depth' surgery which creates the outer appearance of a vagina but, as the name implies, no depth. This operation takes much less time so may be used where other medical conditions preclude 'full' GRS.

Other processes might include:

Breast Implants

Breast development as a result of hormone treatment can vary significantly and tends to be less the later they start hormones. Some may want feminine breasts but don't want to take, or are unable to take, hormones. Others may feel that being able to show a cleavage will increase their self-confidence and want this before they start transition. In such cases, they may seek breast augmentation (BA).

Tracheal Shave

This process shaves the vocal cords and tightens them to raise the pitch of the voice. It reduces the size of the Adam's Apple.

Facial Feminisation Surgery (FFS)

While hormone treatment will tend to soften facial features, some transwomen undergo FFS before or at an early stage of transition to reduce stereotypical male features such as square jawlines, prominent foreheads and high hairlines or to emphasise cheekbones etc.

Female-to-Male Surgical Procedures

Transmen may undergo a double mastectomy to remove the breasts and a hysterectomy to remove the womb and ovaries etc.

Phalloplasty

Phalloplasty is the creation of a penis — usually using donor material from the arm, thigh or stomach.

Time Off for Treatment

The Equality Act 2010 requires that individuals covered by the Protected Characteristic of Gender Reassignment must not be subject to discrimination. It does not specify what time off should be allowed for treatment related to gender reassignment. To avoid being discriminatory, however, it must be equivalent to that allowed for other long-term medical procedures (such as cancer or heart conditions).

If, therefore, someone with cancer is allowed time off for routine hospital appointments, chemotherapy, radiotherapy, counselling etc. and would be allowed a phased return to full-time work following treatment, then a trans individual must be allowed equivalent time off. If, however, a cancer patient was expected to undergo counselling in their own time — then the same could apply to a trans person and it is doubtful if this would be considered discrimination.

Preparing for Surgery

Any surgery involves risks — so it is sensible to ensure that the patient is as fit as possible before that point. This may include losing weight for those who are obese and stopping smoking. Existing medical conditions, such as heart failure, may impact on proposed surgery and will need to be managed. Patients on oestrogen may be advised to come off their hormones up to six weeks before surgery.

Recovering from Surgery

Post-operative care recommendations vary from surgeon to surgeon. For male-to-females in the UK, it was common in the past to remain in bed with very limited movements and no solid foods for several days immediately post-surgery. The 'pack' inserted in the neovagina to prevent it closing up, was typically removed after five days after which the patient could get out of bed and could start taking solid foods. They would usually be discharged, subject to satisfactory recovery, seven days after surgery.

Elsewhere and more recently in the UK, patients are encouraged to remain mobile immediately following surgery and are allowed solid foods much more quickly. Some clinics in Thailand and the USA discharge patients after a shorter stay with recuperation in hotels or elsewhere.

It is important to limit pressure on the abdominal region (and the neo-vagina) and the operation and subsequent recovery put significant demands on the body. Post-operative patients are, therefore, likely to tire quickly and should not try to exert themselves too much. They also need to guard against infections.

Typical guidelines include:

- Avoid strenuous activity for 6 weeks and swimming, cycling or horse riding for 3 months
- Do not bathe or submerge in water for 8 weeks. Showering is OK and pat the areas of surgery dry. Some clinics recommend Betadine solution or a saline solution as a douche.
- Swelling is normal and will gradually diminish
- Some vaginal discharge can be expected for 4-8 weeks and some light bleeding/spotting may occur up to 8 weeks
- Wash hands before and after contact with the genital area and wipe from front to back to avoid contamination from the anal area
- Dilation is important and may be required up to three sessions daily to ensure that the neo-vagina does not close up
- Unless advised otherwise, sexual intercourse can be resumed 3 months after surgery
- Smoking can interfere with the healing process and should be avoided for a month post-surgery.
- Some discomfort or pain is to be expected at first post-surgery.
- For female-to-male patients, normal guidelines apply following mastectomies and hysterectomies. They also need to be aware of issues specifically involved in phalloplasty:

- Wound infections
- Wound breakdown
- Urinary Catheter issues: eg blocked catheter.
- Urinary Tract Infections
- Flap loss where the transferred material does not take
- Pelvic or Groin Hematomas
- Rectal Injury
- Erectile Implant infections

Young Trans People

Increased awareness of transgender issues has resulted in a growing number of young people identifying as trans and seeking treatment. In the UK, cross-sex hormone treatment and surgery are not available until the individual is 16.

This means that they would expect to go through puberty and experience the associated physical changes. These include: deepening of the voice and development of Adam's Apple and facial hair in those assigned male at birth and breast development and menstruation in those assigned female at birth— which are amongst the most obvious causes of distress for trans people.

Puberty Blockers

Puberty blockers defer the onset of puberty until the individual is old enough to commence further treatment — or decides against transition. They may have been prescribed at the onset of puberty.

The outcomes are generally accepted as reversible and without significant side effects.

Whilst they don't eliminate the need for GRS, they can obviate the need for tracheal shaves, facial feminisation surgery, breast augmentation and electrolysis in those assigned male at birth and hysterectomies and mastectomies in those assigned female at birth. They also mean that transwomen's voices don't deepen.

At the time of writing (October 2023) a review is underway regarding the prescribing of puberty blockers which may stop the provision of puberty blockers other than under exceptional circumstances.

Self-harm and suicide amongst young trans individuals

Research undertaken by Stonewall showed that 80% of trans young people who have been bullied have self-harmed and almost half have attempted suicide — despite homophobic, biphobic and transphobic bullying having fallen to 45%.

Addressing LGBT bullying in schools

Mermaids, the support charity for young trans people, Stonewall, the Proud Trust and Diversity Role Models are four of the charities that address LGBT bullying in schools.

Chapter 7 Travelling On: Post Transition/ Surgery

Not all trans individuals undergo surgery but, for many, it is their main focus, if not obsession, for several years and is a major watershed for them. In reality, however, it is not as big a step as social transition.

Once individuals have completed transition, with or without surgery, they may decide to blend into the general population.

8 Stage Process as a Trans Person

Vivienne Cass developed a 6-stage process for individuals' development as Gay[7] A similar process can be applied to trans individuals although I think an 8-stage process is more appropriate (not all individuals will go through all of the stages):

1. **Ignorance**

    Lack of awareness of trans

2. **Denial**

    Refusal to accept that one is trans

3. **Investigation/ Comparison with Others**

    Considers the possibility of being trans; compares their own feelings/ approaches to other trans individuals; identifies options

4. **Tolerance of Possibility**

    Acknowledges that they are probably trans; seeks out trans contacts; explores how they may fit into the trans spectrum

5. **Acceptance of Self**

    Acceptance that they are trans; assesses consequences and, if appropriate, transitions

6. **Pride**

    Is proud of being trans and is open about being so (as far as possible)

7. **Campaigner/ Activist**

    Openly campaigns for trans rights; wears the T-shirts; participates in Pride events.

---

[7] Cass, V. (1979). Homosexual identity formation: A theoretical model. Journal of Homosexuality, 4 (3), 219-235

Chapter 7 Travelling on: Post Transition/ Surgery

8. **Absorption**

    Being trans becomes a less important factor in their life; melds into the background much of the time. They may not tell all new contacts about their trans history.

To be Out or Not?

Even post-transition, being trans does raise a significant question for nearly all transmen and transwomen — do you tell people your history? If so, who do you tell and when do you tell them? The choice should be entirely the individual's. In most circumstances, a trans person's history is irrelevant.

Passing/ Stealth

There is, however, significant debate within the trans community over *'passing'* or living *'stealth'*. Some activists claim that *'passing'* or adopting a *'Cisnormative'* approach is negative (it implies pretending to be something they are not or reinforcing stereotypes) — that trans people should be open about who they are and their history; that this is the route to greater acceptance. They also say that trans people should be *'authentic'*.

There is some truth in those arguments but they ignore the reality that being identified as trans is uncomfortable and may result in verbal or physical abuse — or worse.

A counter argument is that as soon as someone knows an individual is trans, it affects their perception of that individual and can become their most important factor — when, in fact, everyone is made up of vast numbers of facets. There is a case for letting people get to know you as an individual before revealing a trans history. Having got to know the person without initial impressions being coloured by their trans history, it may change their perception of trans people generally.

There is also the question of 'what is authentic?' And do trans people need to be visibly 'out' all of the time to be authentic?

I regularly attend aquarobics sessions at the gym. When you are soaking wet with hair plastered flat, wearing just a swimming costume, it can hardly get more authentic. I dress as I do because that's how I feel comfortable. Most of the time this is in trousers with casual or smart tops (depending on where I may be going). I sometimes wear make-up but probably not if I'm popping out to Sainsbury's for some shopping. In the summer, I may wear a skirt instead of trousers — or even shorts around the house or in the garden. I also like to dress up for special events. I don't see this as 'trying to pass' or being 'Cisnormative'. I do it because it feels right for me as a woman.

Relationships

Telling or not is particularly relevant in close personal relationships. If you tell a potential partner on first contact, there is a very good chance that they will reject you immediately. I had two profiles on a dating site which were identical other than one mentioning a trans history and the other not mentioning it. The latter produced ten times as many responses as the open version.

Chapter 7 Travelling on: Post Transition/ Surgery

If you don't tell them from the start, the relationship may have become important to you. When you do tell them they may feel you have been hiding the truth and reject you and that may hurt much more.

There is also the possibility that if the relationship has become intimate, they may become verbally or physically abusive. A number of transwomen have been murdered by partners who have pleaded that their reaction was a natural one to finding out about the trans person's history.

Many trans people avoid intimate relations rather than risk rejection. Others establish relationships with other trans individuals.

Sex by Fraud

In one case, a Scottish transman was sentenced for 'obtaining sexual intimacy by fraud' for failing to inform two of his girlfriends about his gender history.

Cross Gender Health Risks

NHS notifications of screening are based on recorded gender but trans people can be at risk of conditions based on both the gender assigned at birth as well as their affirmed gender, it is important that they are aware of the need to request additional screening where appropriate. The following information is taken from Public Health England's leaflet Trans01 published July 2017[8].

Breast Screening

Available to transwomen and transmen (if they have breast tissue). It is offered to individuals registered with their GPs as female aged 50 to 70 and carried out every 3 years.

Cervical Screening

Available to transmen. It is offered to individuals registered as female every 3 years from the age of 25 to 49 and every 5 years from the ages of 50 to 65 and to those over 64 who have not had screening since age 50. Transmen, registered with their GP as male, who have not had a total hysterectomy and still have a cervix should consider requesting a test.

Transwomen registered with their GP as female will be invited for screening but do not need it as they don't have a cervix.

Abnormal Aortic Aneurysm Screening

The wall of the aorta can become weak and stretch to form an abdominal aortic aneurysm (AAA). There is a high risk of dying from a ruptured AAA.

AAAs are far more common in men over 65 than women and younger men and the screening programme only invites individuals registered as male. Transwomen are at the same risk as a man and should consider screening. Transmen registered as female will not be invited, those registered as male will be invited and may consider screening even though their risk is lower.

---

[8] Can be ordered from www.gov.uk/phe/screening-leaflets.

Chapter 7 Travelling on: Post Transition/ Surgery

Bowel Screening

Available to transwomen and transmen. Both men and women are routinely invited for screening once at age 55, then at 2 yearly intervals from 60 to 74.

Chapter 8 Trans Issues in Counselling

Many counselling clients come to initial sessions with their 'presenting issue' which may or may not be the underlying concern. The counsellor may then unearth the main issues and the client and counsellor may work through them until they feel they have been resolved. The sessions may be at regular weekly or monthly intervals and are often limited to six or twelve sessions.

This is often not appropriate with trans clients, especially those going through transition and possibly surgery.

They may come to counselling with an initial concern (perhaps about whether they are transsexual or transvestite – or feeling ashamed because of their 'tendencies'); this may be dealt with — but it may not be the end of the client's needs.

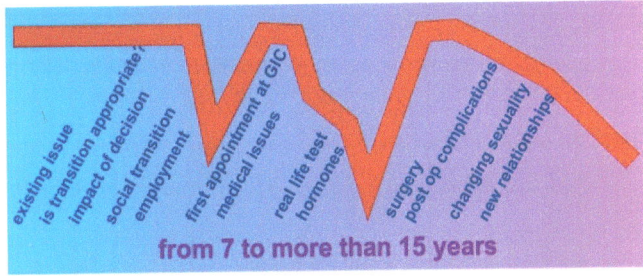

If they transition, they may then be faced with further issues as they continue on their journey:

♦ coming out to family and friends;
♦ referrals to GICs;
♦ transition at work;
♦ possible medical issues,
♦ referrals for surgery,
♦ what to expect post-surgery
♦ and relationships after surgery.

These will occur at different intervals and will continue for a number of years. The client will probably benefit from varied frequencies of sessions; perhaps weekly at first stretching to monthly or even three-monthly as issues are dealt with but reverting to more frequent sessions as new stages are reached in their journey.

As well as the usual range of issues from childhood and medical problems, there are a significant number that are specific to trans people:

Who am I?

Need to 'know myself'

Trans people 'feel different' from an early age and cannot fit into the boxes that society tries to place them.

Chapter 8 Trans Issues in Counselling

Deciding whether or not to transition

Many question for significant periods whether they are cross-dressers or if full transition is more appropriate.

Accepting that they are transsexual

There can be a 'grey' area between transvestism and being transsexual (and, increasingly non-binary and gender fluid). Perhaps 80% of those who eventually decide to transition have previously identified as transvestite. Deciding whether transition is appropriate and, if so, to what extent is crucial!

It should be possible to discuss this with the consultant psychiatrist — but if the individual is going to an NHS Gender Identity Clinic, any 'doubts' may result in the GIC deciding that you cannot be transsexual and stopping treatment. It may take years to decide.

It is also likely that some trans individuals will decide that transition is not appropriate at a particular time but decide years later that it is.

Need to understand why they are trans; why am I the way I am?

Understanding what makes individuals trans helps them to come to terms with the condition.

Is being trans causing other psychological problems — or are other psychological problems making me believe that I am trans?

Where the individual is suffering from other conditions, this can be a valid question. I have experience of a transsexual individual who was in this situation. She had been in and out of hospital for about 4 years and the psychiatrists who were dealing with her seemed uncertain where the truth lay.

Being in the 'wrong body'

A commonly reported feeling expressed by trans people is discomfort with their physical state.

What do I do about being trans? What if I don't do anything?

Dealing with repercussions of suppression

Very few TSs have escaped trying to suppress their gender dysphoria (or cross-dressing if they originally identified as transvestite). 83% of those responding to questionnaires that I had on the internet said they had tried to stop 'dressing' or treatment. If they do try to suppress the feelings, it will lead to stress.

What are the consequences of transition?

I am concerned about starting hormone treatment as they may actually 'tip the balance' between being TV and TS.

Some psychiatrists have used hormone treatment as a diagnostic tool and if an individual is not transsexual, the loss of libido etc can help them to realise that transition is not for them. If someone is borderline, however, the oestrogen could affect areas of the brain and have a small but significant feminising effect which may 'tip the balance'.

Some argue that the effect is psychosomatic and the consequence of having accepted what we are and deciding to do something about it. This does not, however, explain why many experience the opposite effect with a noticeable recurrence of gender dysphoria if we come off hormones (eg for surgery).

Transition

I don't want to transition — I want to feel comfortable as a man

Perhaps 1 in 30 would have preferred to have felt comfortable as a man rather than be transsexual. One of my contacts dreaded seeing the psychiatrist in case he said she was transsexual.

Bereavement/ loss

There can be an experience of bereavement or loss in respect of our birth-sex persona. It may even be worse – a feeling that you have killed your old self.

'Letting the side down' by stopping transition process.

Approximately 80% of the people who saw one of the leading psychiatrists dealing with transsexualism did not undergo surgery — but withdrew from treatment. Nevertheless, some trans people who have started the process feel that they cannot stop when they have concerns.

Being refused the use of 'appropriate gender' single sex facilities

The use of appropriate single-sex facilities is frequently seen as a major stumbling block for individuals transitioning. This results in trans people avoiding the use of such facilities especially until they have undergone GRS.

Need to understand the transition process

There is a myriad of details involved in transitioning. The transsexual individual has to get to grips with these issues. They may not know where to start.

Medical complications

I have been told that I cannot have surgery because there are potential complications

I cannot take hormones because they cause my blood pressure to rise

I cannot take testosterone (f to m) — because I become too aggressive and it affects my heart

Although social transition is usually the most important transition stage, medical treatment to feminise (if AMAB) or masculinise (if AFAB) the body is also very important to many trans individuals. Not being able to undergo that treatment may leave them in limbo.

Fear of failing to achieve requirements for operation (reducing weight, cessation of smoking etc.)

These are very common problems faced by TSs.

Chapter 8 Trans Issues in Counselling

Doctor told me to pull myself together and act like the man I was born to be

My doctor refuses to treat me

Nearly two-thirds of trans people have had problems with medical practitioners due to being trans including one in five GPs refusing to provide any treatment and more than half using the wrong name or pronoun.[9]

Substance Use

A high level of trans individuals use drugs, smoke or have significantly harmful levels of alcohol use. [10]

Frustration over delays in treatment

Cancelled appointments and delays in surgery are quite common on the NHS. Some individuals feel that they are being deliberately prevented from proceeding with treatment

Sausage machine syndrome

One respondent to questionnaires on the internet said "It felt to me that transsexual patients are considered 'sausage meat' to feed into a machine and hope that they came out the other end in reasonable condition. If some emerged deformed — well, so long as there were not too many, that was acceptable".

Dealing with a second puberty during transition

There is often an emotional roller coaster due to the effect of hormones.

Side effects of hormones

Hormones may exaggerate emotions. If the individual is already susceptible to mood swings, then they are likely to be magnified to almost intolerable degrees. If they are relatively stable — then even a 2-3 times increase in intensity might be relatively easy to handle.

Coming off hormones for surgery

It is usual to come off hormones prior to surgery and stay off them for about 1 month afterwards. This causes a further switch in hormone levels; possible recurrence of gender dysphoria, possible erections and night ejaculation; regrowth of facial/ body hair and other symptoms which may be distressing.

Post-operative depression

As well as the usual post-op depression due to residual anaesthetic effects, discomfort etc. Trans people often build themselves up to the operation and become totally focused on it. Once it is over, they actually have a 'hole' in their life.

---

[9] Trans Mental Health Study
[10] Trans Mental Health Study

Fear of surgery (what if I make the wrong decision?) / Fear of post-op complications

Few trans people are totally without any doubts about having the op. There is also the reality that all operations involve risks.

Self Esteem

I'm a pervert/ not normal

Decades of conditioning can make trans people feel this.

Low self-esteem/ belief in self

This problem is not, of course, restricted to trans people.

Being 'failed men'

Transwomen may have failed to achieve many typical masculine attainments and may consider themselves to have failed as men.

Guilt

66% of trans people hid their transsexualism or cross-dressing from their partners. They feel guilt for this deception; and because their partner is now being faced with the breakdown of a marriage and the destruction of a home — often at middle age or later. They may also be depriving children of their father. Guilt may also relate to religious beliefs.

Divine retribution/ punishment for past sins

Many trans individuals have been taught that being trans is against their religious beliefs. They may see setbacks in their lives as punishment from God for their evil behaviour.

Self-harm & Suicide

Prevention of suicide

At one time it was estimated that more than 30% of TSs committed suicide. The Internet has provided far more information and there is far more public awareness of the condition these days. Nevertheless, 84% of respondents to the Trans Mental Health Study 2012 had thought about ending their lives at some point and 48% of them had made at least one attempt.

Relationships

Do I try to merge into the background or admit my past?

This is an ongoing problem. 'If I start to get involved in a relationship, do I tell a potential partner that I have a trans history before we meet; during a first meeting; later or never? If I decide on the former, there is a very good chance that I will either attract men who only want me because I am trans; if I wait — then they may feel I have misled them or been dishonest. I may become emotionally involved and could be badly hurt if my past (or my perceived dishonesty) causes them to reject me'.

How do trans people tell their partner/ children/ parents/ other family members that they are trans?

Apart from the fact that 'coming out' inevitably changes relationships; there may be a perceived possibility that the resultant severe shock might have devastating effects on elderly parents. Yet, if they don't tell them — because the trans person anticipates that they may die before long in any case — will they then start wishing for this to happen?"

Changing relationship with partner

Even if a partner stays with the trans person, the relationship is bound to change. This may be because the TS's own needs and sexuality shift — then they may feel guilty about abandoning a partner who stood by them.

Sometimes this desire to stay together is more about not wanting to leave a safe space; in any event, few wives are able to accept a transitioned 'husband' (and even fewer husbands are prepared to accept that their wife is now a man).

My children do not know what to call me/

"I don't now receive either a Mother's or Father's Day card/ present; they can't call me 'mum' because I'm not their mother. I don't feel comfortable with them calling out 'dad' in the middle of a supermarket. They don't feel comfortable calling me by my Christian name."

Lack of understanding

There is a lack of awareness of what it means to be transgender — and of the implications of that situation. Trans people often find themselves having to educate those who are supposed to help them[11].

Making others accept that I am transsexual

This might range from close family & friends to work colleagues and even GPs. It is also a major fear when seeing psychiatrists for assessments and continuing treatment by Gender Identity Clinics.

I am constantly rejected because I am trans

Whilst this might well be the case, it is also possibly because the individual is not easy to get along with. That may be due to their worries about their condition – or they may just not be a pleasant individual.

Post Transition

Inability to give birth/ not being a 'complete' woman

Sterile women may also share this issue.

---

[11] Trans Mental Health Study 2012

Planning for future

The operation is not the end of the process. It's the end of the beginning. For the trans individual to be able to move on, we need to have some idea of where we will be going afterwards with our lives.

Escaping the ghettos

During transition, many trans people will limit social interaction to relatively safe environments such as support groups or gay scenes. However, these can become ghettos and most need to escape and become assimilated into the general public. Taking the first steps of going into 'normal' areas can be very scary.

Coming Out

Dealing with ridicule

Few trans people escape ridicule and no matter how confident they are, they can still find it painful. One adverse incident outweighs hundreds of positive comments.

Remaining Stealth

Passing in public

Many trans people are concerned about '*passing*' — not being identified as trans. This is discussed earlier in Passing/ Stealth. They may feel guilty about wanting to 'pass'.

Sexuality Issues

Changes to sexual orientation

Around 32% of TSs experience a change in sexual orientation during transition. It is quite common for transwomen to shift from an attraction to females before commencing transition towards an attraction to men by about a year post-operative. During this time, it is quite likely that the individual might experiment sexually.[12]

Gay transvestite or transsexual

Being transvestite may be seen as a perversion; as may being gay. Some trans people may consequently think 'I like dressing as a female — and I like sex with men, so I am a 'normal' female'. A significant number of gay transvestites seek 'legitimisation' of their 'double perversion' by identifying as transsexual — they see it as a medical condition.

Isolation/ support

Isolation

Unless the individual is in touch with other TSs, the isolation can be intense. This can lead to other problems: alcohol/ drug abuse and offences resulting from these

---

[12] Questionnaires I had on the internet

problems which makes getting employment even more difficult and lead to increased isolation.

Issues from upbringing

Handling looking back at the 'wrong childhood'

When trans people talk to friends about childhood experiences, they have to decide whether to speak openly about having grown up as a boy and having been involved with the cubs and scouts etc. and remind their friends that they used to be male (or vice versa) — or avoid speaking about their past.

This also applies in other groups where the trans history is not necessarily known and the conversation relates to husbands/ wives/ partners.

Employment

Cannot get a job because of being trans

It is illegal to discriminate in this way — but trans people have to prove that it was due to the fact that the individual is transsexual. In some cases, it may not have been.

Other

Help others understand trans issues

There is still a huge amount of ignorance about transsexual issues in spite of massive steps forward in recent years.

Jealously — of others who have fewer problems

Why me? What did I do to deserve this? Life is unfair.

The unknown

The unknown is always scary, but many clients can avoid going there by staying in their safe zones. A trans individual may have decided to transition and there is no option but to go into the unknown.

Special Issues

Intersex

Intersex people may have health and social issues arising from their difference. They may also have medical needs that arise directly from early medical interventions they have been subjected to. Examples include:

- Feeling and being different
- Not fitting into binary gender
- Complications over personal relationships
- Inability to be a biological mother or father in some cases
- Subject to comments about genitalia and, in common with other trans individuals, their appearance such as excess body and facial hair, voice, size and male pattern baldness which can necessitate wearing a wig

Chapter 8 Trans Issues in Counselling

- Being excluded from certain binary gender-specific activities and clubs
- The trauma of undergoing up to 17 gender tests administered by an endocrinologist and other tests with gynaecologists and dermatologists.
- Absence of specific protection under the Equality Act 2010.

Non-binary/ gender-fluid

The world is basically set up for a binary view of gender and scant regard paid to those who don't fit within this scheme. This will produce a range of specific issues including the lack of legal recognition and protection; the absence of appropriate facilities; being unable to join gender-based organisations.

Non-binary and gender-fluid individuals may even face discrimination from other trans individuals especially when considering campaigning for rights.

Transvestite Issues

Transvestites may also share some of the issues faced with being transsexual — and a range of specific concerns of their own. This may include uncertainty over legal status; which facilities to use; where they can get changed if they want to remain stealth at home; risk of partners/ family finding out about their activities. Not least may be concerns that they may eventually decide that they are transsexual rather than transvestite and need to transition.

There may also be confusion about the difference between being transvestite and gender fluid as both may be seen as switching roles/ gender presentation.

Body dysmorphia — brain's body map

In extreme cases, the individual may want or need to have the 'offending' part removed. This may be linked to the phantom limb syndrome experienced by amputees. In the case of amputees, the brain map of the body includes the amputated limb; perhaps in the case of body dysmorphia, that limb is missing from the body map — in the case of transsexual individuals because the body map reflects the true gender rather than the physical sex of the individual. I had one client referred to me by another counsellor who was entirely happy in his chosen gender but felt totally uncomfortable having a penis and wondered if he was transsexual.

Many, but not all, transsexual individuals can't stand the fact that they have inappropriate body parts and can't even look at them. Others prefer to have the parts removed so that their body can be made as appropriate a match as possible to their gender.

Issues for Elderly Trans People

Dementia

With dementia causing the loss of most recent memories first, it is likely that some elderly trans people will end up remembering childhoods in their birth gender but not later years and may be confused about their current situation in a different gender.

Carers

Elderly trans people may need support as they get older. This may create issues if those providing the care are unaware of trans issues – including Cross Gender Health

Chapter 8 Trans Issues in Counselling

Risks (Chapter 7). If the trans individual has socially transitioned but not undergone surgery they may need to 'out' themselves to the carers,

Therapeutic Approaches: Holistic and Eclectic

A holistic and eclectic approach is, I believe, essential when dealing with trans clients. They may need:

- Counselling to deal with:
    - issues that have arisen from their background
    - problems that will arise from the transition process
    - any complications that might arise during transition
    - coming to terms with living completely in their new role
    - coming to terms with possible changes to their sexual orientation
    - break-up of relationships
    - handling 'death of old persona'
- information about:
    - how to decide if they are transsexual
    - where to go for treatment
    - what to do if their GP refuses to help
    - private psychiatrists that deal with trans clients
    - what to expect from hormone treatment
    - possible surgeons
    - what to expect after surgery
    - causes of trans conditions
    - sources of support
- advice on:
    - how to handle 'coming out' to family, friends & colleagues etc.
    - legal rights
    - how to arrange changes of names and official records

Only a part of this would be considered to be counselling. However, the reality is that the information needs are critical and will make a major difference to the state of mind of the trans person. Attempting to deal solely with the 'feelings' around the issues is like prescribing aspirin for a headache caused by eyestrain. It may provide temporary relief — but just as glasses would eliminate the eyestrain and, therefore, the headaches; information about and treatment of the condition will eliminate some of the underlying problems that lead to the need for counselling.

Chapter 9 Partners and Families

This book focuses mainly on supporting the trans individual and dealing with the issues that they may face. But their family will also face issues.

Partner/Husband/ Wife/Spouse:

The individual's partner may feel that the individual has been cheating on them. If that had been with another person then they might have been able to fight back but when the person they are competing with is inside their partner that becomes almost impossible.

I've had trans clients who said that they would do anything to avoid hurting their partners or children but this is unlikely to be true as they would rarely halt their transition or stop cross-dressing in the case of transvestites. It may be possible to suppress their desires for a while but they will usually resurface at some stage.

The partner may also wonder if the marriage ever meant anything or was it always a sham? Were they not enough of a woman (or man) for their partner? As one put it "If my husband was really always a she, then were we ever really an 'us'[13]?"

Many trans individuals go through periods of suppression or denial of their feelings and it is often during such periods that they get married and have families. They often think that their trans period was simply a phase that they've grown out of especially as they enter their late teens/ twenties. They may also have felt that getting married would be the answer to their drives.

Some trans people may tell their partners of their cross-dressing/ trans feelings at an early stage in the relationship. The partner may feel that they can accept cross-dressing providing it remains in private and does not embarrass them. Others may actively participate in the cross-dressing. They don't anticipate that it will develop further and, in many cases, it doesn't.

It tends to be when the trans person identifies as transsexual and decides that they need to transition that the issue presents completely different challenges.

They then have to decide if they are going to stay together and, if so, the basis of any future relationship — emotional as well as physical.

Some partners will say that they still love the individual regardless of their gender and that their feelings haven't changed. In other cases, the relationship may cease to be physical and be for companionship.

If the couple does remain together, it may make the partner question their own sexual orientation. This may present issues of faith if they have been taught that same-sex relationships are sinful.

---

[13] Lisa Jaffe Hubbell Los Angeles Times, 21 Jul 2015

Chapter 9 Partners and Families

In the case of trans men, they may have identified as lesbian rather than cross-dressing. They may be in a relationship with a woman. If they now identify as male, does that relationship now become heterosexual? If so, how does their partner feel about it? How do gay/ lesbian friends now feel about a male in their circle?

If they stay together and the trans person transitions, there may be concerns about 'what the neighbours/ friends/ work colleagues etc. and wider family will say.'

If they don't stay together, they are faced with the usual consequences of divorce with the loss of homes and possessions and the anticipated secure future that the partner may have been counting on.

Most partners of trans people struggle to find support for themselves. 'I looked for peer-reviewed academic articles on how healthcare professionals could help the families of trans people through their own transitions. I couldn't find any; I still can't.[14]'

Trans groups have tried to set up support networks for the partners of trans people but the groups are often seen as biased (we probably are) and focused on trying to keep the partnership together.

Children

Any children may be faced with what they now call the parent who has transitioned. Is it reasonable to expect them to call their former dad 'mum' (or vice versa) — or does that detract from their natal mother?

Do the children pretend to friends and schoolmates that their transitioned parent has left their life/ died? Or how do they tell their school or workmates?

Will other family elders demand that there is no contact between the transitioned parent and the children? This has occurred in strict religious groups where it is felt that further contact would contaminate the children and result in their friends' parents preventing their children from having contact with the children of a trans person.

Children may also be confused — can they trust anything that the transitioning parent told them?

Siblings

Some described it as having had bereavement but with no grave to grieve over. Others are reluctant to make an effort to address the trans person by their new name or appropriate pronouns. 'It's your problem — why should I have to make adjustments?'

Siblings may also blame the trans person for health issues faced by their parents after a trans person has come out to them and prevent the trans person from seeing nephews or nieces with whom they had previously had excellent relationships.

Parents

Parents may wonder if they had done something wrong or if they were to blame in some other way. They may wonder if they should have picked up on signals during childhood.

---

[14] Lisa Jaffe Hubbell Los Angeles Times, 21 Jul 2015

Chapter 9 Partners and Families

If the trans individual is still a child, they may wonder what they can do — or if they should do anything at all. They may wonder if 'encouraging' cross-gender play or dressing/ behaviour will make it more likely that the individual will grow up to be trans.

They may wonder if they will grow out of a phase they are going through.

Further information can be obtained from Mermaids[15] the charity that supports young trans people and their families.

---

[15] http://www.mermaidsuk.org.uk/

Chapter 10 Case Studies

Some of the following cases are or have been clients; others were significant in my decision to study counselling.

A

This is an article written by a client in 2009.

A change of mind; Realising your inner-self through counselling.

The following account is my honest experience.

I had reached the age of 44 and was taking stock of things. On one hand I had built a very successful business, had a very strong marriage, a lovely home and sports car, I was respected within the business community and was generally well liked as a typical man's man. Women often flirted with me and guys liked my company. It seemed as though I had achieved everything I set out to do... Or had I?

On the other side of things, I had failing health, everything from a bad back, putting on excess weight, feeling sick, feverish, headaches, I had also developed breathing difficulties like asthma at night time making a good night's sleep impossible. I was constantly at my local NHS Doctors and frequently doing physiotherapy but I seemed to be getting worse.

My mental Health had deteriorated to an all-time low. Fronting as successful happy business man by day and by night desperately trying to understand what was going wrong with me. I even thought I was losing my mind. I couldn't work it out.

I knew from the age of 4 that I was transgendered but had always generally managed to cope with this. I had had a few problems with this over the years but had learnt to conceal it. I wondered whether this was where my problems were rooted.

I used the transgendered support networks for advice. The Unique group in Wales recommended a counsellor called Helen Dale who was based and worked in the Manchester area. I contacted her and made an appointment in the LGF building in Manchester. This was January 2008. I wasn't too sure of what I was trying to achieve or how it would work out but I was desperate to do something. On meeting Helen, she explained that she was a post-operative transsexual and was now happy in her new role and keen to help others through counselling. However, she made it clear that she was not in this to encourage other transgendered people to transition but solely to help them with their issues. She stated that everyone is different and everyone finds different ways to come to terms with their own concerns.

I agreed a contract and stated that my 'goal' was a better quality of life than that I had. I had agreed to visit on a monthly visit on a Thursday for a 1-hour session. The first few visits passed quickly but I only felt comforted by talking about my past but didn't feel that I was making any real changes to my problems. I discontinued seeing Helen after about 7 months. The months that followed without seeing Helen became very worrying in terms of personal health and mental stability. My health deteriorated very rapidly, I even thought at one point I was going to die. They were the darkest days of my life.

I contacted Helen again and regained my association with the support groups. Helen accepted me without question and focused on moving forward rather than going over why I stopped attending. I slowly started to stabilise and sessions started to deepen. I slowly realised that I had no identity I was self-fabricated, I somehow had become what I thought everyone wanted from me, rather than being myself. I was basically in denial which was compounding my problems and stalling any progress. I gained enough confidence to talk to my GP about my health and it was he that suggested that my ill health could be attributed to my gender identity issues. He made a referral to the local NHS mental Health team. This I ran alongside my counselling with Helen, drawing on the counselling to support myself through the sometimes-difficult NHS sessions. The NHS process for me was frustrating and complicated but I was determined to get through it out of self-preservation. After a series of blunders by the NHS I made some serious complaints and was only then finally referred to the specialist unit at Charring Cross in London. During this time, I worked very hard between my sessions with Helen to improve my 'mindset'. I realised the more I relaxed in role as female the stronger and more empowered I felt about myself. My health started to improve I started to even exercise, lose weight and even feel happy!

It had taken me years to finally realise what my problems were and what I may have to do to try to change the way I live my life. I currently am contemplating a real-life experience and am in the process of making permanent adjustments to my life. I am finding life a real challenge right now but one I am looking forward to embrace rather than dread.

I now believe that I have surpassed my original expectations of what counselling could provide for me. I believe that I am now beginning to live my life rather than just improve the quality of it. I will use the counselling service that Helen provides until I feel 'complete' or 'together' enough to have worked through all my issues. I feel as though I'm getting close to the end of this process and am even thinking of how I may help others like myself in the future.

I don't believe the NHS provide any help in this area of support but instead focus on the 'obvious' and the 'accountable' within its treatment regime. There is a big gap between someone being unsure of one's gender to knowing what you want to do about it. That is a shame as people like me end up costing the NHS much more because we are not recognised in terms of treatment. Instead, we end up statistically listed under many other areas hidden as suicides, offenders and prison numbers or totally reliant on the state as broken people. I only navigated through this system because I was well supported, educated, experienced, patient and had significant resources to support me. The counselling provided the vehicle to get me to where I needed to be. I can't stop thinking of those who are not so fortunate....

This former client is now openly living as a female and helping other trans individuals including running a support group and acting as an advocate in meetings. Since ceasing to be a client, both she and her wife have become friends.

B

Body Dysmorphic

I was volunteering at the Lesbian and Gay Foundation (now LGBT Foundation) in Manchester when another member of the counselling team asked if I could see one of their clients who was wondering if they were transsexual as they wanted to have their genitals removed.

When I met with the client, it became apparent that they were entirely happy with their gender and had no wish to transition — but wanted to have surgery. We explored the concept of body dysmorphia and the possibility that he was experiencing the reverse of "phantom limb" syndrome. That seemed to make more sense to him and he concluded that he was not transsexual.

C

C was estimated to be in her early 30s when I saw her in February 2001. She was a teacher at an all-girl school. At that time, she anticipated transitioning and wanted to be prepared for any issues that she would face as a consequence. She decided to put counselling 'on hold' until she decided to proceed.

D

D was mid 40s when I first saw her; she was married with children from an earlier marriage. She first came to see me in January 2001 to try to decide whether or not she was transsexual.

After a few sessions, she decided to seek treatment and approached a clinic in Manchester. She was assessed by them as 'probably secondary transsexual'. The clinic sent a letter to her GP recommending hormone treatment. The GP refused to prescribe them 'because they are not approved for men'.

Major issues have involved potential break up of marriage; coming out to children; problems with GP; housing; and employment.

In Oct 2001, D's wife was away on holiday when it struck D how much she stood to lose by continuing with transition. She decided that she had to stop transitioning and revert to male mode to avoid losing her wife.

She was referred back to me in 2014 by which time the marriage had ended and her children had grown up. She has now transitioned at work and undergone surgery and apart from issues with one line manager has enjoyed support from colleagues.

E

E was a contact via an Internet chat line. She has not been a counselling client — but it was concerns over her that contributed to my decision to start counselling training.

Chapter 10 Case Studies

She was isolated and needed someone to talk to. I invited her to visit me at my flat. At this time, I identified as TV rather than transsexual and anticipated that E was also TV.

It became apparent to me that this was not the case when we chatted. She did not, however, wish to be transsexual. She said that if she was transsexual then she could not expect her wife to remain with her and she would not wish to live without her wife.

She eventually went to see a specialist who confirmed my view that she exhibited signs of being transsexual. He prescribed hormone treatment. Her GP refused to convert the private prescription to an NHS one and told her 'You were born a man; you will die as a man. That was how God made you and how you are meant to be. You need to pull yourself together and live as the man you are meant to be'.

Her e-mails became less and less frequent then ceased.

F

F was a young person assigned female at birth who identified as male. He was anxious to start on puberty blockers to prevent the development of breasts and subsequent surgery to remove them. Unable to get an appointment with the NHS quickly enough due to long waiting lists, the family went to a private service and were able to obtain the puberty blockers. The individual was then concerned that until he was prescribed hormones, his physical development would fall behind his male peers.

Chapter 11 Legal history

In February 1970, Justice Omerod ruled in the April Ashley divorce case that male-to-female transsexual people were 'male' for the purpose of marriage. In 1973, the Court of Appeal ruled that it was 'unacceptable situation in law' for a person to be a man for one purpose and a woman for others.

For the next 20+ years, trans people were in social and political oblivion with no legal protection. They were subjected to sensationalist press exposures and ridicule. This started to change in the 1990s with the establishment of Press for Change — which campaigned for changes to the law.

P v S & Cornwall County Council 1996

P was dismissed by Cornwall County Council because she was transsexual. The UK government contended that discrimination against individuals undergoing gender reassignment was not covered by the EEC directive 76/207/EEC on the principle of equal treatment for men and women as regards access to employment, vocational training and promotion because it only applied to men and women and she would have been dismissed whether she was male-to-female or female-to-male.

The European Court of Justice ruled that discrimination based on gender reassignment should be compared with persons of the sex to which the individual belonged before reassignment not whether a trans person would have been treated differently if they were male-to-female compared with female-to-male.

Sex Discrimination Act — Gender Reassignment Regulations 1998

These Regulations extended the Sex Discrimination Act 1975 to cover discrimination on grounds of gender reassignment in employment and vocational training, following the judgement of the European Court of Justice in Case No. C-13/94 P v S and Cornwall County Council. (Repealed in 2010 — replaced by the Equality Act 2010)

Gender Recognition Act 2004

The Gender Recognition Act was published in 2003, received Royal Assent in 2004 and became effective in 2005. It was reviewed in 2018 to extend the coverage of the Act and simplify the process for obtaining a Gender Recognition Certificate. The government decided not to implement the recommendations of the review other than reducing the cost of a GRC.

Summary of Implications of the Gender Recognition Act

- Transsexual individuals who meet certain criteria can apply for a Gender Recognition Certificate.

- If granted, that certificate gives those individuals legal recognition (with a few exceptions) in their 'acquired' gender.
- They also receive new birth certificates
- And are entitled to marry in their 'acquired' gender role.

These qualifying criteria are:
- has or has had gender dysphoria
- has lived in the acquired gender for the preceding two years (for the first 6 months after the bill, there was a 6 years qualification period to enable a backlog to be dealt with)
- intends to live in the acquired gender permanently

Surgery or an intention to have surgery is **not** a prerequisite for recognition. This reflects the fact that some individuals are unable to undergo surgery and for female-to-males, the surgery involves several different procedures.

There are some significant limitations:

- Before the Marriage (Same Sex Couples) Act 2013, if the individual was married in their birth gender, the existing marriage had to be dissolved before the individual could obtain a GRC. This is no longer the case but the spouse needs to agree to the marriage continuing after the acquisition of a GRC. As some do not want to be in a 'same-sex' marriage, this is considered a 'right of veto' by some trans individuals.
- Female-to-male transsexual men who are between 60 and 65 years of age who receive pensions as they are still currently female in law would lose their entitlement to that pension if they accepted a GRC before their 65th birthday. This is no longer relevant as pension ages have been harmonised.
- Individual Church of England clergy can decline, on the basis of conscience, to perform marriages for those marrying in their acquired gender. (Similar to the position regarding divorce)
- Individuals who do marry in their acquired gender role will have to tell their partner of their transition or the marriage may be annulled.
- Sporting bodies may have the right to restrict participation where there may be an advantage (due to physique from a masculine body before transition) or a danger to other competitors. (The International Olympic Committee does now accept transsexual competitors providing they had surgery more than 2 years earlier to allow the body to feminise and the male muscle structure to be reduced. Despite this ruling, several sports have implemented bans on trans women competing against other women.)

Prohibition of Disclosure of Information

Section 22 of the Gender Recognition Act 2004 deals with the "Disclosure of Protected Information". It states that:

> "It is an offence for a person who has acquired protected information in an official capacity to disclose the information to any other person"

Protected information is:

Information about an application for a Gender Recognition Certificate (GRC)

Or, if the individual has a GRC, information about an individual's previous gender.

There are exemptions to this prohibition on disclosure. These include:

If the information does not identify the person

If the person has agreed to disclosure

If the individual disclosing the information does not know that the person has a GRC

The disclosure is in accordance with the order of a court or tribunal

Disclosure is for the purposes of proceedings before a court or tribunal

Disclosure is for the purpose of investigating or preventing crime.

The above exemptions were extended in Statutory Instrument 2005-635 (see Appendix 2) to include certain circumstances involving:

Disclosure for purpose of obtaining legal advice

Disclosure for religious purposes

Disclosure for medical purposes

Credit reference agencies

Insolvency

Unlawful disclosure is a strict liability **criminal** offence. There is no pleading of 'reasonableness'. The Data Protection Act requires organisations to take reasonable steps to protect data; the GRA demands that the data is protected without regard to how reasonable the steps required might be.

Goods & Services 2008

Made it unlawful to discriminate on the grounds of gender reassignment in the provision of goods and services. (Repealed in 2010 — replaced by Equality Act 2010)

Civil Partnership 2004 & Marriage (Same Sex Couples) Act 2013

The Civil Partnership Act allowed same-sex couples to register their partnerships. The Marriage (Same Sex Couples) Act allows same-sex couples to marry — but more importantly, for the trans community, it allows a couple who are already married to remain married even if one of the partners goes through gender reassignment and obtains a Gender Recognition Certificate (provided the spouse agrees). Previously they would have had to be divorced or the marriage annulled before the individual could obtain a full GRC.

Equality Act 2010

The Equality Act 2010 includes 'Gender Reassignment' as one of the 'Protected Characteristics'. In theory, this gives transsexual individuals the same protection and priority in issues of discrimination as any of the other eight characteristics. In practice, it seems unlikely that organisations will devote as much time and effort into training and awareness on trans issues as they do around other aspects.

Chapter 11 Legal History

It also provides no protection at all for other individuals under the trans umbrella who do not 'propose to undergo, are undergoing or have undergone' gender reassignment unless the discrimination occurs because they are perceived to be transsexual (or gay) or because it is due to association with someone who is transsexual (or has one of the other characteristics).

Chapter 12 Discrimination and Hate Crime/ Incidents

Jokes

Jokes may seem harmless but they can impact on individuals. For example, in a quiz show on BBC the 'celebrities' were asked what they would not want to find on a date. One responded 'big hands' — clearly referring to trans individuals and making it clear that he did not see trans women as 'real women'. He and the BBC saw this as a trivial issue — but the difficulty in establishing relationships is a major concern to many trans people.

Transphobic jokes (or any other discriminatory jokes) also imply that it's OK to laugh at minority groups; if it's OK to laugh at them, it's OK to treat them differently and, if it's OK to treat them differently, it's OK to discriminate. Jokes, therefore can lead to much more serious forms of discrimination and abuse.

There has been an 11% increase in transgender hate crimes from 2021-2 and a 186% increase since 2019 against an overall reduction in hate crime.

Abuse

- 73% of respondents to a Press for Change survey experienced harassment, with 10% being victims of threatening behaviour when out in public spaces.
- General confidence in the police among members of the trans community is quite high, however, 18.5% of those who actually had interactions with the police felt they were not treated appropriately.
- 47% of trans people do not use public social or leisure facilities for fear of discriminatory treatment — by being refused access or having their access limited in some way.
- 20% of respondents felt informally excluded from their local community and neighbourhood since their transition
- Asked to leave church. — have been told that 'people wouldn't understand and would feel uncomfortable if I attended'.
- Being transferred from one person to another in the accounts department of the Burlington Macdonald Hotel in Birmingham, which LAGIP had used for a conference, I heard:
    'Helen Dale, the man who thought he was a woman'
    The hotel said it wasn't intended to offend!

Physical Assaults

Many trans people experience physical assaults. The Office of National Statistics says that trans people are 22 times more likely to be murdered than the average.

Criminal damage

I have personally experienced criminal damage including broken windows, graffiti and 'tranny' scratched on my front door. I was forced to cover my windows with plastic sheeting to stop the stones from breaking the glass. At one time there were more than 20 holes in the plastic.

Sporting

Trans people experience discrimination in many sports and not just those where there may be a perceived advantage for transwomen due to skeletal/ muscle structures.
- "I shoot air pistols and want to compete. But the international governing body ISSF ban trans shooters from their competitions until 2 years after final surgery to minimise gender advantage in line with IOC rules.
- The thing is that shooting was a mixed sport in the Olympics from 1968-1992 so gender advantage doesn't come in to the sport yet trans shooters are still banned by the ISSF.
- IOC recommendation is that once a transwoman has been on hormones for two years she should be allowed to compete in women's events; transmen are not restricted from competing in male events.

Media Portrayal

- Trans people are frequently portrayed as freaks & deviants or programmes focus on stereotypes such as a transwoman looking in a mirror, putting on make-up or on surgical procedures. They are rarely shown to just be individuals getting on with their lives.

Goods & Services

In spite of legal rights, trans people often experience discrimination in the provision of goods and services:
- Refused admission to local swimming pool.
- Was told by the manager of the establishment that my sort weren't allowed in because whenever he's allowed my sort in there's always trouble.
- At a beauty college where I was receiving electrolysis the college principal intervened and told me I could not be treated there because I had not had GRS and the college was for women only.
- Visiting Weymouth, group of 4 trans women, empty restaurant, said they were full and closed, shoved us out, locked the door, re-opened for business five minutes later after we had left.
- Asked to leave a pub when with another trans woman who was just starting her transition.

Chapter 12 Discrimination and Hate Crime/ Incidents

- I was refused a membership at a local self-defence group for women
- I was barred from a pub for using the ladies after I had GRS and even with 'a note from my doctor'.
- I was told — 'we don't serve your sort here'.
- One health club refused me membership due to my being pre-op.
- Refused access to an all-women's disco; then refused admission to a gay Country and Western club (owned by a well-known trans woman) because it was men only!
- Told by male police officer that I chose to be trans. When I tried to correct him, he handcuffed me and read me my rights.
- I was attacked in front of a police officer, who simply shrugged when she witnessed the assault (as if to say 'You brought it on yourself, the way you look'); then she turned around and walked off.
- Local beat officer made inappropriate comments about me after I'd been subjected to threatening behaviour in my home by a neighbour.
- Was asked to disclose if pre- or post-op before being searched.
- They were informed I was pre op by 3rd party and I was searched by 2 men.
- I was so traumatised by this search and the comments that when released I went to Beachy Head to commit suicide.

At Work

- 42% of trans people prevented from transitioning because of fears it would affect their employment status
- 1 in 4 trans people made to use inappropriate toilet facilities
- 10% experienced verbal abuse
- 6% physically assaulted
- 25% felt obliged to change jobs because of harassment & bullying
- I had to leave job after transition due to being told I would have to continue using male facilities such as toilets and changing rooms.
- One week I was told I was the best worker in the computer workshop; 2 weeks later I was told my assignment wasn't being continued.
- Some application forms require trans people to out themselves immediately (through requests for previous names)
- Some diversity monitoring forms also breach the GRA

Changing Documents

- Banks and other financial institutions and Universities often fail to promptly change the details on people's records.
- Many organisations, including universities, the police and health authorities now falsely claim that no change of name, gender or pronouns can be made without a Gender Recognition Certificate.
- 21% of respondents' GPs did not want to help with transition

- 6% refused to help
- 17% of respondents have had experience of doctor or nurse who did not approve of gender reassignment and hence refused services
- 29% felt that being trans affected the way they were treated by healthcare professionals
- Being moved from one hospital to another after a heart attack; the nurse told the ambulance driver that I had had gender reassignment — which had no relevance whatsoever.
- Told to find another hospital to deal with for transition-related treatment as it was too inconvenient for Salford Royal Hospital to comply with GRA on unlawful disclosure of protected information.

Schools

Some 64% of young trans men and 44% of young trans women will experience harassment or bullying at school, not just from their fellow pupils but also from school staff including teachers

Family

- 45% of respondents reported family breakdown which was due to their cross-gender identity.
- 37% are excluded from family events and have family members who no longer speak to them because they have transitioned to their acquired gender
- 36% of respondents (294 of 803) have family members who do not speak to them anymore because of their transition or preferred/acquired gender.
- The resulting isolation for the trans person (and sometimes their partners) can leave them extremely depressed and anxious.
- my priest sent me to be re-baptised. I am married, and I have a disabled son I am now on anti-depressants.
- ...my grandparents, who are very close to me, are very old and I don't think they can take the shock. That was the reason why I wanted to wait; I don't want to break their hearts.
- My parents know about my transitioning and they have told me in no uncertain terms that they don't want anyone else in the family to know. So essentially when I am living in my acquired gender, I'll never see my family again.
- At family functions I have to appear in my birth gender to save embarrassment to my family.
- For many trans people facing a crisis in their partner relationship, which may result in the loss of their home and severe financial problems, the lack of family support may often be the straw that breaks the camel's back, and can lead to severe personal crises that can result in attempted suicide.

Chapter 13 Employment

Diversity Benefits Business

A diverse workforce is good for business. It produces different ideas and approaches that the organisation can benefit from — whereas a homogenous group fails to identify new opportunities and can become stale in its approach. It resists change and goes into decline.

All businesses need to attract the very best staff into all its roles regardless of sex, gender reassignment, age, religion or belief, race, sexual orientation, disability, marital status, maternity and pregnancy etc. The absence of discrimination on the grounds of these 'protected characteristics' is not just a requirement under the Equality Act 2010, it makes sound business sense.

The Government Equality Office says:

'It is in an employer's interest to secure the best possible applicants in order to gain or retain competitive advantage or be able to offer the best possible service. We know that significant barriers exist for trans people seeking employment but there are various steps that employers can take to:

- Be thought of as a "good employer" within the trans community;
- Attract applications from suitably qualified trans job seekers;
- Ensure that the recruitment processes do not present barriers to trans applicants; and
- Ensure that recruiting managers respond to, and assess trans candidates appropriately.'

Under the EA 2010, organisations are required to make 'reasonable adjustments' to meet the needs of disabled staff. While being trans is not a disability, there, similarly, may be some adjustments that organisations need to make when employing trans individuals.

The issues involved may depend on whether the individual is a current employee – or starting work with the organisation in their 'acquired gender'. Some issues will apply in both cases as well as when the individual identifies as non-binary or gender fluid.

Organisations in the public sector should refer to the a:gender *'Workplace Guide'* which is written specifically for the Civil Service but should be applied across the public sector or the Government Equality Office publication *'The Recruitment and Retention of Transgender Staff Guidance for Employers'*.

Monitoring Gender & Gender Identity

If you don't know the breakdown of your staff or customers, how can you tell if you are providing the services they require? As far as gender is concerned, you should not just offer male/ female as options; nor should 'transgender' be included as a further option as most trans individuals identify as male or female. It is appropriate to offer 'intersex', 'non-binary' or 'gender fluid' as alternatives to 'male' and 'female' and offer the option of 'other' where individuals can indicate their preferred description. Questions about gender identity should be separate from those about gender (and sexual orientation). This can be achieved by asking 'Is your gender different to that assigned at birth' with yes/ no options. You may also ask 'what pronouns do you use?'

Where this (or other sensitive diversity) information is monitored, organisations should consider doing so by computer using entry forms that only the subjects themselves can access. This is a relatively simple and inexpensive procedure with common HR systems such as Oracle. The organisations should then be able to produce reports from the data without identifying individuals. Any reports producing less than say 5 that could reveal individuals should produce a null return. For example, 'number of IT Project Managers who are Trans' at Greater Manchester Probation would have produced the answer of 1. As I was the only IT Project Manager, this would have 'outed me' (if I hadn't already been known to be trans).

Single-sex facilities

Agreement may need to be reached about the use of single-sex facilities such as toilets and changing rooms to ensure appropriate privacy for all staff.

Under the Equality Act 2010, an individual falls within the Protected Characteristic of "Gender Reassignment" if they propose to undergo, are undergoing or have undergone a process of gender reassignment. They do not have to be under medical supervision for this to apply. The Gender Recognition Act 2004 does not require an individual to undergo surgery to be legally recognised in their 'acquired gender'.

It would be inappropriate to expect an individual that has started transition to continue to use the single-sex facilities of their birth gender or to be restricted to the use of accessible facilities such as toilets.

If necessary, to ensure privacy for all staff, it may be necessary for workplaces to consider the installation of individual changing and showering cubicles.

Non-binary / gender-fluid

Whilst most trans people identify principally or exclusively as male or female, an increasing number are identifying as non-binary or gender fluid. Although not specifically covered by either the Gender Recognition Act 2004 or the Equality Act 2010 at the time of writing, a review of the GRA scheduled for 2018 considered extending the remit in accordance with the report of the House of Commons Women and Equalities Committee report on Transgender Equality 2015-16. Although the government decided not to implement the recommendations, it is good practice to consider a wider application of any trans policies. This includes the use of single-sex facilities.

There is no 'one size fits all' solution to which facilities a non-binary or gender fluid person should use or which part of a dress code they should follow and the individual's views should be taken into account. It is not acceptable to simply say 'this individual has not legally changed their recognised gender through a Gender Recognition Certificate so remains legally of their birth sex and must use facilities and follow the dress code for their legal sex". Nor is it acceptable to base decisions on whether the individual has male or female genitalia.

As explained elsewhere, many trans people choose not to undergo surgery or obtain a GRC for valid reasons.

Organisations should question why they have communal single-sex facilities and consider how these could be made into gender-neutral spaces with individual cubicles. In the meantime, they may be able to identify facilities that can be designated as Gender Neutral or, more simply, just marked as 'Toilet' or 'Changing Room' or 'Shower'.

Support for the Individual

Individuals who are transitioning need support. This may be in the form of counselling or peer-to-peer support. There are a number of organisations that provide support — although many of these are combined transvestite & transsexual and usually more biased towards TV than TS; a:gender has also been established as a pan civil service network for trans individuals.

Transitioning In Service

Where an individual transitions within an organisation, it will often not be possible to remain anonymous. It is an essential part of the gender reassignment process for the individual to live in role as part of 'Real Life Experience'. The change of role may produce reactions from colleagues some of which may be hostile. This may include deliberate abuse, jokes, exclusion from social activities, persistent use of previous names, persistent misuse of gender pronouns, refusal to work with the individual and intrusive questioning.

Awareness training may be useful to minimise adverse reactions but if they continue, then the employer must protect the individual who is transitioning.

Stay in role

Some individuals transitioning will wish to remain in their current role. This may necessitate notifying contacts within and outside the organisation of the change or, in some cases, changing their specific tasks so that they stay in the same role but handle different accounts for example.

Redeployment

The other option is to redeploy the individual to a different section or even office. This is unlikely to be 100% effective as other colleagues may move jobs later or visit the new office etc. The individual should not be pressured into accepting redeployment.

Disclosure – colleagues / external contacts

The individual concerned must be involved in any communication plans. They must be happy with the extent of any disclosure. Some will be happy to announce their plans to everyone in the organisation; others will prefer to keep it within their immediate team.

It is important that the announcement is supported by a clear statement from the Chief Executive or a senior manager that any discrimination against the individual will not be tolerated.

Support

The organisation's trans or LGBT support networks (where they exist) are likely to provide a valuable source of support for the individual. They may also benefit from counselling to help with the issues that may arise or from a mentor with experience of transition.

Post transition, the organisation should ensure that the individual's line manager or another designated individual monitors any issues that may occur.

Planning

'Failing to Plan is Planning to Fail' is an adage that applies to transition within the workplace. The key issues will include:

- When will transition occur?
- What will need to change?
    - Name badges
    - Security pass
    - IT systems
        - Computer log-on
        - Email addresses
        - Team listings
        - File access lists
    - Payroll records
    - HR records
    - Telephone lists
    - Tax & NI records
        - Who will notify HMRC & DWP?
    - Pension details
    - Uniforms or other occupational clothing?
- Who needs to know?
- How will they be told?
- Is there likely to be media interest?
    - If so, how will this be handled?
        - Pre-emptive news release or one available for release if coverage occurs?
        - Arrangements to direct all enquiries to professional PR support?
        - Arrangements for the individual to stay away from home if media attention becomes too intrusive?

Timing

The timing of the change should be agreed with the individual. Some trans individuals prefer to make the change after a natural break such as a bank holiday or annual leave. Others may be happy not to have a break. In either case, the organisation should ensure that the transition is as smooth as possible with any security passes, computer log-ons etc arranged ready for the individual's return to work.

Record changing

Records should be changed ready for transition. However, it should be noted that Section 22 of the Gender Recognition Act 2004 prohibits disclosure of 'Protected Information' in an official capacity except as covered by specific exemptions detailed in the Act and extended in Statutory Instrument 2005/ 635. Refer to Chapter 11 Legal and Chapter 15 Appendix 1 and 2.

Whilst individuals going through transition will not normally have qualified for a Gender Recognition Certificate, they may well do so while working for the organisation and the rules governing unauthorised disclosure will include ALL records relating to that individual.

This could mean, for example, that giving access to new members of staff within HR or Payroll to IT systems that contain information about the individual's previous names or refers to them by gender-specific pronouns that are no longer applicable could breach Section 22. Even if the individual gives permission for details to be shared on a wider basis, that permission can be withdrawn at any time.

Trawling back through records at a later date to remove or amend data that might be affected would be a very difficult and time-consuming task.

Passes

Security Passes should be made available as soon as possible ideally before the individual starts work in their acquired gender. This may not be possible if the pass includes a photograph of the subject.

Existing records that can't be changed

Any existing records that cannot be changed including contracts and minutes of meetings should have access restricted to those who need to see them. The access lists should be agreed with the subject to avoid unlawful disclosure of protected information if the individual later acquires a Gender Recognition Certificate.

IT log-ons

IT log-ons, email accounts, directory listings, file access lists and any other IT records that might disclose the individual's gender history must be changed.

New applicants

Genuine Occupational Qualifications

The GEO states:

Very occasionally, there may be genuine occupational factors that legitimately restrict applicants. This is known as a 'Genuine Occupational Qualification' (GOQ).

Chapter 13 Employment

Very careful consideration should be given before applying a GOQ. Such restrictions are rare and, if wrongly applied, unlawful.

Recruitment

It is unlawful to discriminate on the grounds of 'gender reassignment'. If an applicant has a Gender Recognition Certificate they are 'for all purposes' the gender listed on that certificate and there is no obligation to disclose their gender history unless there is a requirement to do so for security vetting purposes. In such cases, the disclosure should only need to be made to those undertaking the vetting and should not be revealed without permission or a court order.

Gender/ Titles / Previous Names

Asking for gender/ titles/ previous names on application forms, the need to provide references or proof of qualifications may discourage transgender individuals from applying as they would need to disclose their gender history if their previous names were gender specific. This can amount to indirect discrimination and employers should take steps to avoid this possibility.

Asking for this information may also result in a breach of Section 22 of the Gender Recognition Act 2004 if the applicant has a Gender Recognition Certificate, states this on the application form and the form is then seen by other people.

Greater Manchester Probation put in place a system to avoid this situation and included the following statement on the guidance notes that accompanied application forms.

Guidance for Transgendered Applicants

'We welcome applications from individuals who identify themselves as transgendered. We provide designated contacts within our HR Department to assist you with the application process. Please read the following notes prior to completing your application

1. *Monitoring Data Form. If you do not wish to identify yourself as transgendered you may leave this section blank. If you wish to return the Monitoring Data Form in a separate envelope you may do so.*
2. *You will not be asked to disclose previous names until an offer of employment is made. At this point you will be asked to complete a form detailing previous names. This will be treated confidentially and will only be held by the designated individuals, who are aware of the Gender Recognition Act 2004 in respect of disclosure of protected information. GMPA treats information about transgendered applicants and staff as though it is covered by the Gender Recognition Act 2004 whether or not the individual has applied for or has been granted a Gender Recognition Certificate.*
3. *Successful candidates may be required to obtain Criminal Records Bureau clearance. There is a designated process for transgendered individuals to follow in relation to this and assistance can be obtained from the named contacts.*

Whilst the wording now needs to be updated, this showed an awareness of trans issues and that the organisation welcomed applications from trans individuals.

Employers should also consider mentioning in the Job Description that applications from trans (and other minority groups) are welcomed.

In terms of gender, just offering male/ female as options excludes those that are non-binary or gender fluid. It may also be seen as asking for the individual's legal gender rather than how they now identify.

It would be more inclusive to offer an option for the individual to write in the gender with which they identify if other than a binary male/ female. Organisations should ask why they need to know an applicant's gender in any case.

Similarly, with titles, there should be an opportunity to select 'other' and write in the person's preferred title. Again, does the organisation need this information?

Stealth

An individual joining the organisation in their acquired gender role may choose to keep their history private. This is sometimes known as being 'stealth'. There may be some records that cannot be secret such as tax and national insurance and pension records. Where it is necessary for this information to be shared, it must be kept to a minimum.

Disclosure

Whether or not an individual has a GRC should not affect the extent to which information is kept confidential. The difference is that disclosure of 'protected information' about an individual with a GRC except as allowed under the GRA is a criminal offence. The information would also be covered under the Data Protection Act as 'sensitive information' and 'reasonable steps taken to protect it'.

The steps detailed within the GRA could be considered 'reasonable'.

Harassment

The employer has an obligation to protect the individual from harassment. Redeployment against the individual's wishes should not be used to remove them from any sources of harassment.

Misnaming misgendering

Persistent misuse of gender pronouns or previous names is harassment and must not be permitted.

Dress code

Where uniforms / clothing are provided for staff, the appropriate gender items should be provided on the same basis as normal replacements.

Where the organisation operates a dress code the individual should follow the dress code for the gender with which they identify.

Searching

Discrimination law no longer contains the previous specific bar to prevent trans people without gender recognition from searching individuals of their acquired gender[16].

Police and Criminal Evidence 2012 guidelines on searching trans people state that someone identifying as female and living predominantly in that gender should be searched by another female and one identifying as male should be searched by a male. Where the individual might be subject to routine or other searches, the organisation should follow the same guidelines.

Neither the Equality Act nor PACE specifically refer to non-binary or gender-fluid individuals. If it becomes necessary to search a non-binary or gender-fluid individual, the individual's wishes as to who carries out the search should be respected.

Medical Adjustments/ Absences

Many trans employees may need a number of different medical interventions requiring absence from work and these are outlined below. Such absence is covered by Section 16 Equality Act 2010 which states that an employer must not treat a person absent because of gender reassignment less favourably than they would treat:

- absence due to sickness or injury
- absence for some other reason if it is not reasonable to do so

Public sector organisations have an additional 'Public Sector Duty' to advance equality. It requires organisations to have regard to the need to remove or minimise disadvantage and meet the different needs of those with a protected characteristic. This allows and encourages employers to take positive action that removes the significant disadvantage that would inevitably be incurred by staff undergoing gender reassignment. The Equality & Human Rights Commission guidance recommends an entirely separate process for dealing with gender reassignment absence.[17]

GIC Appointments

Individuals undergoing gender reassignment may require time to attend appointments at GICs or with a private specialist. Typically at three-monthly intervals, these appointments will be a necessary part of the process and failure to attend could affect the individual's treatment.

Speech Therapy

One of the effects of male puberty is the breaking of the voice. This process is irreversible (except by surgery) and is unaffected by female hormones. The voice can be trained to increase the pitch and intonations by practicing a range of techniques taught during speech therapy.

---

[16] A vs Chief Constable of West Yorkshire Police.

[17] A:gender Workplace Guide.

Electrolysis

Transwomen usually undergo laser/ pulsed light or needle electrolysis to eliminate facial hair growth. Laser/ PL treatment is usually provided at four to six weekly intervals for many months. There may be some redness following laser treatment and it may take some days for the blackened roots of hairs treated during the sessions to fall out and the individual may be self-conscious about their appearance at this stage. Needle electrolysis may require a few days' hair growth ready for treatment and, again the individual may be self-conscious at this stage. It may be appropriate to negotiate working timetables during this period.

Hair Transplants

Some transwomen with male pattern baldness may consider hair transplantation although this has to be funded privately.

Hormone Treatment – Implants/ Injections

Some hormone treatment involves implants or injections which may not be self-administered and may need to be done by medical practitioners during normal working hours.

Surgery

Many of the procedures undertaken by trans people involve major surgery with significant post-surgery recovery times. Such absences should not be regarded as 'sickness' triggering performance review processes.

Return to work/ Phased returns

Staff who have been away from work for significant periods may need a planned 'return to work' programme in line with arrangements for other staff recovering from major surgery.

Performance issues

The stresses involved in transitioning, the physical changes and the impact of hormones on the emotional state of the individual may sometimes impact on the subject's performance. Allowance may need to be made for this in the same way that it would be for staff being treated for cancer or other major conditions.

Transgender Awareness Training

Transgender awareness training for colleagues may be a key element in facilitating a smooth transition and acceptance of the individual.

Chapter 14 Bibliography

The following books provide further information on transgender issues. Some may no longer be in print but might be found second hand.

Risks Myths and Sexuality

Edited by Karen Buckley and Paul Head

joint social services and probation service book looking at sexuality and service users. Includes one chapter on transgender offenders.

Russell House Publishing

ISBN 1898924368 / 978- 1898924364

True Selves

Mildred L Brown and Chloe Ann Rounsley

USA focused book aimed at those involved with transsexual people especially families and counsellors.

Josey-Bass A Wiley Imprint

ISBN 0-7879-0271-3 (cloth) 0-7879-6702-5 (paperback)

As Nature Made Him

John Colapinto

An examination of the case where Dr Money convinced the parents of a baby boy whose penis had been destroyed during circumcision as a girl and exposes Money's subsequent claim that the case had been successful as untrue.

Harper Perenial

Transgender Warriors

Leslie Feinberg

An alternative approach to being trans on the basis that it should be regarded as a third sex and that transsexuals should not collude with simple bi-polarisation of gender.

Beacon Press 1997

ISBN-10: 0807079413

ISBN-13: 978-0807079416

The Transgender Debate

Stephen Whittle

Small booklet by one of the Vice Presidents of Press for Change containing facts and snippets about being trans

Brainsex

Ann Moir and David Jessel

An examination of the difference between male and female brains and resultant behaviour

Mazndarin 1991

ISBN-10: 0749305258

ISBN-13: 978-0749305253

Stand-Up for Yourself

Shelley Bridgman

Excellent autobiography of a transwoman.

Stand-up Publishing 2014

ISBN-10: 0957571208

ISBN-13: 978-0957571204

True Colours

Caroline Paige

In 1999, Caroline became the first ever openly serving transgender officer in the British military. Already a highly respected aviator, she rose against the extraordinary challenges placed before her to remain on the front line in the war on terror, serving a further sixteen years and flying battlefield helicopters in Bosnia, Iraq and Afghanistan

Biteback Publishing 2017

Trans Britain

Edited by Christine Burns

Trans Britain chronicles the emergence from the shadows in the words of those who were there to witness a marginalised community grow into the visible phenomenon we recognise today: activists, film-makers, broadcasters, parents, an actress, a rock musician and a priest, among many others.

Unbound 2018

Trans Mental Health Study 2012

Report of a study by Jay McNeil, Louis Bailey, Sonja Ellis, James Morton and Maeve Regan

www.scottishtrans.org 2012

Tale of Two Lives

(A Funny Thing Happened on the Way to the Palace)

Helen Dale

My own autobiography; published 2018

ISBN 978-1-9996329-7-7 Paperback edition with black/white illustrations

ISBN 978-1-9996329-9-1 Hardback edition with colour illustrations

Transgender Tales

– Adventures and Misadventures on a Journey from Transvestite to Transsexual

Helen Dale

A Collection of items I wrote in 1997-9 when I was deciding whether I was transvestite or transsexual; includes a diary over that period; items on coming out to friends, family and at work, some short stories and other humorous anecdotes

ISBN 978-1-9803629-1-5 (paperback)

Chapter 15 Appendices

Appendix 1. Gender Recognition Act 2004 Section 22

Prohibition on Disclosure of Information

Section 22 of the Gender Recognition Act states:

(1) It is an offence for a person who has acquired protected information in an official capacity to disclose the information to any other person.
(2) "Protected information" means information which relates to a person who has made an application under section 1(1) and which-
    a. concerns that application or any application by the person under section 5(2) or 6(1), or
    b. if the application under section 1(1) is granted, otherwise concerns the person's gender before it becomes the acquired gender
(3) A person acquires protected information in an official capacity if the person acquires it-
    a. in connection with the person's functions as a member of the civil service, a constable or the holder of any other public office or in connection with the functions of a local or public authority or of a voluntary organisation,
    b. as an employer, or prospective employer, of the person to whom the information relates or as a person employed by such an employer or prospective employer, or
    c. in the course of, or otherwise in connection with, the conduct of business or the supply of professional services.
(4) But it is not an offence under this section to disclose protected information relating to a person if-
    a. the information does not enable that person to be identified,
    b. that person has agreed to the disclosure of the information.
    c. the information is protected information by virtue of subsection (2)(b) and the person by whom the disclosure is made does not know or believe that a full gender recognition certificate has been issued,
    d. the disclosure is in accordance with an order of a court or tribunal,
    e. the disclosure is for the purpose of instituting, or otherwise for the purposes of, proceedings before a court or tribunal,
    f. the disclosure is for the purpose of preventing or investigating crime,
    g. the disclosure is made to the Registrar General for England and Wales, the Registrar General for Scotland or the Registrar General for Northern Ireland,

Appendices

    h. the disclosure is made for the purposes of the social security system or a pension scheme,

    i. the disclosure is in accordance with provision made by an order under subsection (5), or

    j. the disclosure is in accordance with any provision of, or made by virtue of, an enactment other than this section.

(5) The Secretary of State may by order make provision prescribing circumstances in which the disclosure of protected information is not to constitute an offence under this section.

(6) The power conferred by subsection (5) is exercisable by the Scottish Ministers (rather than the Secretary of State) where the provision to be made is within the legislative competence of the Scottish Parliament.

(7) An order under subsection (5) may make provision permitting-

    a. disclosure to specified persons or persons of a specified description,

    b. disclosure for specified purposes,

    c. disclosure of specified descriptions of information, or

    d. disclosure by specified persons or persons of a specified description.

(8) A person guilty of an offence under this section is liable on summary conviction to a fine not exceeding level 5 on the standard scale.

Appendices

Appendix 2. Statutory Instrument 2005-635

The Gender Recognition (Disclosure of Information) (England, Wales and Northern Ireland) Order 2005

Made	9th March 2005
Laid before Parliament	10th March 2005
Coming into force	4th April 2005

The Secretary of State, in exercise of the powers conferred upon him by section 22(5) and (7) of the Gender Recognition Act 2004, hereby makes the following Order:

Citation, commencement and extent

1 - (1) This Order may be cited as the Gender Recognition (Disclosure of Information) (England, Wales and Northern Ireland) Order 2005 and shall come into force on 4th April 2005.

(2) This Order extends to England and Wales and Northern Ireland only.

Interpretation

2. In this Order -

"the Act" means the Gender Recognition Act 2004; and

"the subject", in relation to any protected information, means the person to whom the information relates.

Disclosure for purpose of obtaining legal advice

3 It is not an offence under section 22 of the Act to disclose protected information for the purpose of obtaining legal advice.

Disclosure for religious purposes

4. (1) It is not an offence under section 22 of the Act for a person who acquired protected information in an official capacity in relation to an organised religion to disclose information to any other person acting in such a capacity if the conditions set out in paragraphs (2) and (where applicable) (3) are met.

(2) The first condition is that the disclosure is made for the purpose of enabling any person to make a decision -

(a) whether to officiate at or permit the marriage of the subject;

(b) whether the marriage of the subject is valid or should be annulled or dissolved;

(c) whether to admit or appoint the subject -

(i) as a minister of religion,

(ii) to any employment, office or post for purposes of an organised religion,

(iii) to any religious order or community associated with an organised religion, or

(iv) to membership (or any category of membership) of an organised religion;

(d) whether any admission or appointment mentioned in sub-paragraph (c) is valid or should be suspended, terminated or revoked; or

(e) whether the subject is eligible to receive or take part in any religious sacrament, ordinance or rite, or take part in any act of worship or prayer, according to the practices of an organised religion.

(3) The second condition is that, if the disclosure is made for the purpose of enabling any person to make a decision of the kind mentioned in paragraph (2)(c), (d) or (e), the person making the disclosure reasonably considers that the person to whom the disclosure is made may need the information in order to make a decision which complies with the doctrines of the religion in question or avoids conflicting with the strongly held religious convictions of a significant number of the religion's followers.

(4) It is not an offence under section 22 of the Act for a person who acquired protected information in an official capacity in relation to an organised religion to disclose protected information to any person responsible for supervising him in relation to a decision of the kind mentioned in paragraph (2).

Disclosure for medical purposes

5. - (1) It is not an offence under section 22 of the Act to disclose protected information if -

(a) the disclosure is made to a health professional;

(b) the disclosure is made for medical purposes; and

(c) the person making the disclosure reasonably believes that the subject has given consent to the disclosure or cannot give such consent.

(2) "Medical purposes" includes the purposes of preventative medicine, medical diagnosis and the provision of care and treatment.

Appendices

(3) "Health professional" means any of the following -

(a) a registered medical practitioner;

(b) a registered dentist within the meaning of section 53(1) of the Dentists Act 1984;

(c) a registered pharmaceutical chemist within the meaning of section 24(1) of the Pharmacy Act 1954 or a registered person within the meaning of article 2(2) of the Pharmacy (Northern Ireland) Order 1976

(d) a registered nurse;

(e) a person who is registered under the Health Professions Order 2001 as a paramedic or operating department practitioner;

(f) a person working lawfully in a trainee capacity in any of the professions specified in this paragraph.

Credit reference agencies

6. - (1) It is not an offence under section 22 of the Act to disclose protected information if -

(a) the disclosure is made by or on behalf of a credit reference agency;

(b) the information consists of information contained in an order of a court or tribunal; and

(c) if the credit reference agency has been informed that a full gender recognition certificate has been issued to the subject, the disclosure also contains that information.

(2) It is not an offence under section 22 of the Act, when making a disclosure under paragraph (1), also to disclose protected information obtained from an electoral register.

(3) "Credit reference agency" has the meaning given in section 145(8) of the Consumer Credit Act 1974

Insolvency

7. - (1) It is not an offence under section 22 of the Act to disclose protected information if -

(a) the disclosure is made by or to a relevant officeholder;

Appendices

(b) the disclosure is necessary for the relevant officeholder to perform functions under the Bankruptcy (Scotland) Act 1985, the Insolvency Act 1986, the Company Directors Disqualification Act 1986, the Insolvency (Northern Ireland) Order 1989 or the Company Directors Disqualification (Northern Ireland) Order 2002; and

(d) if the person making the disclosure knows or believes that a full gender recognition certificate has been issued to the subject, the disclosure also contains that information.

(2) "Relevant officeholder" means -

(a) a person acting as an insolvency practitioner within the meaning given by section 388 of the Insolvency Act 1986 or article 3 of the Insolvency (Northern Ireland) Order 1989;

(b) the official receiver within the meaning given by section 399 of the Insolvency Act 1986 or article 2 of the Insolvency (Northern Ireland) Order 1989, in whatever capacity he is acting; or

(c) the Accountant in Bankruptcy within the meaning of the Bankruptcy (Scotland) Act 1985.

Signed by authority of the Secretary of State

Cathy Ashton

Parliamentary Under-Secretary of State Department for Constitutional Affairs

9th March 2005

Appendix 3. Transition Check list

The following checklist is a composite but mainly based on one in the Government Equalities Office 'The Recruitment and Retention of Transgender Staff' 2015

Who needs to know?

Action	Who will tell them?	When?	Done
HR Department/ Business Partner			
Senior Manager			
Line Manager			
Others (list any people that need to know)			

Planning the Future

You	
Your new name (in full, if known)	
Your Role	
Line Manager	
Name	
Position	
Location	
Contact details	
Mentor	
Name	
Position	
Location	
Contact details	
Medical Advisor	
Name	
Position	
Location	
Contact details	

Informing colleagues/ friends/other contacts

Friends	
Who will tell Friends?	
How will this be done?	
Will you be there?	
When will this be done?	
Where will it be done?	
What information will be provided?	
Immediate Team	
Who will tell immediate team?	
How will this be done?	
Will you be there?	
When will this be done?	
Where will it be done?	
What information will be provided?	
Other colleagues on same site	
Who will tell other colleagues on the same site?	
How will this be done?	
Will you be there?	
When will this be done?	
Where will it be done?	
What information will be provided?	
Other colleagues within organisation on other sites	
Who will tell other colleagues at other sites?	
How will this be done?	
Will you be there?	
When will this be done?	
Where will it be done?	
What information will be provided?	
Other external contacts	
Which external contacts will be informed?	
Who will tell external contacts?	
How will this be done?	
Will you be there?	
When will this be done?	

Transition Check List

Where will it be done?	
What information will be provided?	

Preparation for first day post transition

When will this be?	
Will you continue in same role or change roles? If changing roles what will the new role be?	
Are YOU ready?	
Is your uniform/ wardrobe ready?	
Are colleagues ready?	
Is additional support in place for you and loved ones?	
Are there any Media concerns? If so, who is responsible for the plan to deal with this?	

Changing everything into your new identity

Item	Who will do this?	When?	Done
Name Badge			
Security Pass			
Business Cards			
External website biography/ details			
Telephone directory			
IT log-on			
e-mail address/ account			
File/ Directory access lists			
Intranet details			
Work-based social media			
Union membership			
Staff association membership			
Pension scheme			
Tax office			
National Insurance			
Uniform stores data			
Certificates/ awards changed to new name			
Professional Association memberships changed to new name			

Medical appointments and absences

Reason	Dates

Details of planning meetings

Date	Comments	Actions	Date of next meeting

Appendix 4.   Disclosure Agreement

Where organisations need to pass on information about a trans individual, there should be a disclosure agreement such as below:

Section 22 of the Gender Recognition Act 2004 prohibits the disclosure of 'protected information' except under specified circumstances. Protected information relates to an application for a Gender Recognition Certificate or, if the individual has a GRC, to information about their previous gender. [*insert name of counsellor/ organisation*] treats such information about trans individuals as 'protected information' whether or not the individual has, or is known to have, a Gender Recognition Certificate.

This could prevent the counsellor from referring the client to other services that might be appropriate including referring the client to any support groups. The client gives permission for the counsellor/organisation to disclose 'protected information' where necessary to obtain support for the client from other agencies and services. This permission to remain in force until the client gives notice in writing withdrawing that permission.

Where 'protected information' is passed on it will be to named individuals who have been advised of their obligations under the GRA not to disclose it further without permission from the client.

Appendix 5. Brain Sex Test

These are a few sample questions from the questionnaire I've used during face-to-face workshops. Whether the actual individual questions matter may be debatable – but the fact is that the scores do consistently show a difference between the male and female responses – and the few male to female trans individuals' scores have been in the female range.

1	When reading a map or street directory you:							
	Have difficulty and ask for help	a	☐	Turn it around to face the direction you are going	b	☐	Have no difficulty reading maps or street directories	c ☐
2	You are cooking a complicated meal with the radio playing and a friend phones. Do you:							
	Leave the radio on and continue cooking while talking on the phone	a	☐	Turn the radio off, talk and keep cooking	b	☐	Tell them you will call them back when you've finished cooking	c ☐
3	You are in an unfamiliar place and someone asks where north is. You:							
	Confess you don't know	a	☐	Guess where it is after a bit of thought	b	☐	Point towards north without any difficulty	c ☐
4	You've just heard a new song by one of your favourite artists, Usually, you:							
	Can sing some of the song afterwards without difficulty	a	☐	Can sing some of it if it's a simple song	b	☐	Find it hard to remember the tune - but might recall some of the words	c ☐
5	You're in a hotel room and hear the distant sound of a siren. You:							
	Couldn't identify where it's coming from	a	☐	Could probably point to it if you concentrate	b	☐	Could point straight to where it is coming from	c ☐
6	You go to a social meeting and are introduced to seven or eight new people. Next day you:							
	Can easily picture their faces	a	☐	Would remember a few of their faces	b	☐	Would be more likely to remember their names	c ☐
7	You want to go to the country for a holiday; your partner prefers a beach resort. To persuade them, you:							
	Tell them sweetly how you feel and that you love the countryside	a	☐	Tell them if they go the country, you'll be grateful and will be happy to go to the beach next time	b	☐	Use the facts: the country resort is closer, cheaper, and well organised for sporting and leisure activities	c ☐
Scoring								
	Total number of "a's"			Total number of "b's"			Total number of "c's"	
	score **15** points per "a" total "a" score			Score 5 points per "b" total score			Deduct 5 per "c" total score:	
	Add total score for "a"s to total score for "b"s then deduct total score for "c"s							
	Total of "a" score + "b" score minus "c" score:							
	Please indicate your gender:			male: ☐	female: ☐		other: ☐ (please state)	

Appendix 6. Brain Quadrant Test

There are NO RIGHT or WRONG answers.

Tick those answers that apply to you; don't think too much about each reply, your first reaction is likely to be most appropriate

Section 1 LF

- ❏ I prefer to have the final say in family money matters
- ❏ I am logical and tend to think in straight lines
- ❏ I love machines and enjoy using tools
- ❏ I like delegating and giving orders
- ❏ I like to be able to measure my success objectively, it's not enough to just be happy about what I am doing
- ❏ I feel comfortable working with figures
- ❏ I enjoy verbal arguments; I like to get my ideas across
- ❏ I tend to take responsibility for big decisions
- ❏ I am good at technology
- ❏ I value effectiveness in other people
- ❏ People often look to me for leadership
- ❏ If there is a problem, I can usually see what is causing it and come up with an answer
- ❏ I am good at managing money
- ❏ I enjoy DIY
- ❏ I believe thinking is more important than feeling

Section 2 LB

- ❏ I don't like having my routine disturbed
- ❏ I find filing, sorting and labelling relaxing
- ❏ I am uneasy with ambiguity and uncertainty
- ❏ I think rules are important and should be adhered to
- ❏ I always read the instruction leaflet before I use a new appliance
- ❏ If I have to do something tricky, I am happiest if I have an established protocol to follow
- ❏ I put my social commitments in my diary and stick to them
- ❏ I have a place for everything and everything in it's place
- ❏ I think people should keep their emotions under control
- ❏ I am reliable and loyal
- ❏ I enjoy doing repetitive tasks
- ❏ I always tackle tasks one step at a time
- ❏ I like working with details
- ❏ I uphold traditional values
- ❏ I am reliable and thorough in my work

Section 3 RF

- ☐ I use a lot of hand gestures when I talk
- ☐ I like to work on several things at once
- ☐ I often come up with new inventions
- ☐ I often rely on hunches to solve problems
- ☐ I get some of my best ideas when I am not thinking about anything in particular
- ☐ I am very energetic
- ☐ I am artistic
- ☐ I get excited by "off the wall" ideas
- ☐ I always "file" things in stacks rather than in cabinets
- ☐ I tend to be more interested in the "big picture" rather than the details
- ☐ I can always see in my mind's eye how to arrange a room or pack a car boot in order to get everything in
- ☐ I have a sense of humour that has got me into trouble sometimes
- ☐ I am good at ball and computer video games
- ☐ I loathe routine tasks

Section 4 RB

- ☐ I think co-operation is the way to get things done not conflict
- ☐ I tend to reach out and comfort people's body language
- ☐ I love to sing, dance and listen to music
- ☐ I think personal growth is something worth working at
- ☐ I think feelings are more important that thoughts
- ☐ My family and relationships are the most important things in my life
- ☐ I automatically watch people's faces when I am talking to them
- ☐ I know instinctively what people are thinking
- ☐ I feel uneasy when people are arguing around me
- ☐ I am good at making other people feel enthusiastic
- ☐ I think you can measure success by how happy you are feeling rather than what you achieve
- ☐ I think spiritual values are more important than material things
- ☐ I often touch people spontaneously when I talk to them
- ☐ I am good at interpreting body language
- ☐ I cry easily at sloppy films

Brain Quadrant Test

Count scores for sections:

1	
2	
3	
4	

Plot the scores on the chart:

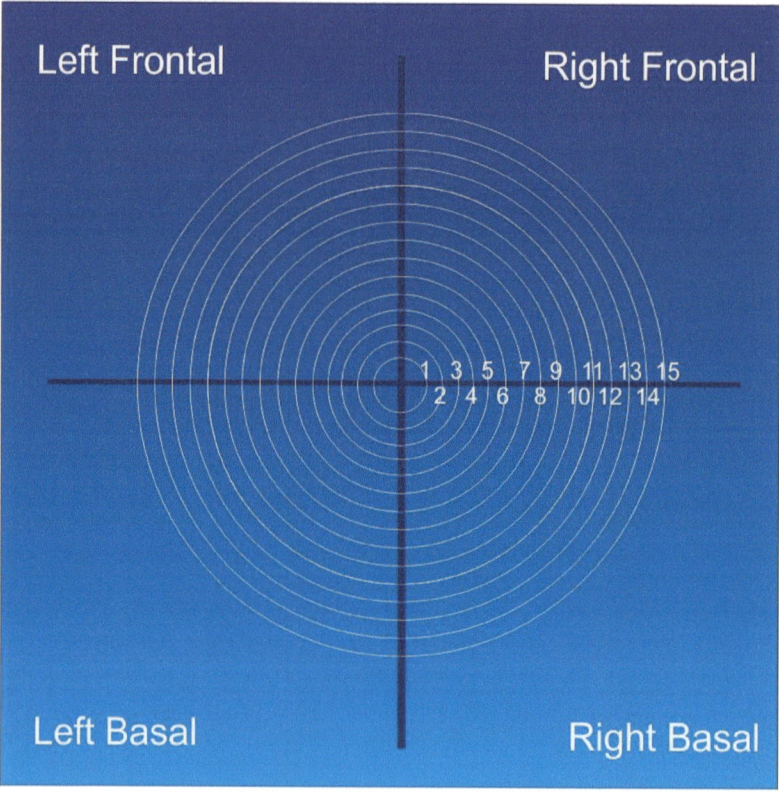

Also by Helen Dale

For more information about how it feels to be trans the following books look at the issues from different angles

A Tale of Two Lives

(A Funny thing happened on the way to the Palace)

Inspirational story of award-winning trans activist, writer, trainer and counsellor: Helen Dale.

Having grown up as a RAF Brat and keen scout, dreaming of being a pilot in the RAF, she concealed a secret for decades before accepting, in 1998, that she needed to transition.

Losing one job as a consequence, Helen joined Greater Manchester Probation in 1999. As the first openly trans employee nationally she provided awareness training for probation and prison staff and others and became the de facto lead on trans issues.

She persuaded LAGIP, the then Lesbian and Gay staff association, to extend its membership criteria to include trans and spent several years as chair. She also helped to found a:gender - the UK pan-Civil Service trans support network and was made an honorary life member when she retired in 2015. Helen served on local and national diversity boards and chaired a trans charity in Manchester as well as training as a counsellor.

Her work was recognised with several awards including a Butler Trust Award presented by HRH Princess Anne at Buckingham Palace.

"A Tale of Two Lives" tells how she came out to family and friends and how that might have been handled better! It also covers her life after transition, embarking on a range of activities: learning to scuba dive, qualifying as a yacht skipper, fire breathing, diving with sharks - including Great Whites - and holidaying around the world as part of a group or on solo trips showing that being trans is no barrier to living a full life.

Now available with colour Illustrations

ISBN

Paperback: (b/w illustrations):   978-1-9996329-7-7

Hardcover (colour illustrations):   978-1-9996329-9-1

what people have already said:

"an excellent read and filled in some of the gaps in your eventful life. It was a brave thing to write it but I would not expect anything less from you"

Also by Helen Dale

"I've read the book and found it very interesting, down to earth, no holds barred, and for me personally extremely helpful in understanding a close relative in a similar situation. Well done, I look forward to the next one."

"I loved this book and as my son is experiencing some of the same issues it gave me insight. I also bought the book for him which I think helped, though he has chosen not to transition. He chose instead to tell his closest friends and felt able to do that."

"A book about journeys and self-discovery and how to weather life's ups and downs. Fascinating insights into Helen's transition story richly peppered with the fullness of family, friendship, work and really living life to the full. Yes, Helen you have made a difference."

"I really enjoyed this book which covers the very interesting life story of Helen. It's a really good read and keeps you interested as well as explaining more about the TV/TS community and the struggles they can face.

Highly recommended"

"I loved this book and as my son is experiencing some of the same issues it gave me insight. I also bought the book for him which I think helped, though he has chosen not to transition. He chose instead to tell his closest friends and felt able to do that."

Transgender Tales

Adventures and Misadventures on the Journey from Transvestite to Transsexual

An online diary Helen kept between 1997 and 1999 when she first moved to Salford. She chatted to lots of other trans people on line, many of whom had never been anywhere "dressed". So Helen invited them to visit and go down Manchester's Gay Village. This tells the story of those trips and others that she made with Vanity Club UK — a TV/TS club.

It also tells of her thoughts over that period when she started by identifying as transvestite but began to wonder if she was actually transsexual and if she would eventually need to transition permanently. There are descriptions of how Helen came out as trans to two of her oldest friends, at work and to her family — and the consequences of those steps.

It also includes:

- three stories that she wrote at the time for Northern Concord's magazine "Crosstalk" under the name Helen Williamson,
- A poem "Can You Tell Me What I Am?" which was written when she was questioning if she was TV or TS
- other humorous anecdotes from the period.

What readers say:

"Some great short stories about the dilemmas of being a TV in the early 80s 90s. The diaries reveal a hidden community proudly remembered for its peer support, mentoring and deep friendship. full of spirit and life."

ISBN 978-1-9996329-1-5

Also by Helen Dale

Novels:

Summer Dreams

"Summer Dreams" is an authentic story of the transgender community and illustrates the wide range of trans people's experiences, the problems, prejudices and fears that they face (and some of their own prejudices) — and the fact that being trans is just one facet of their lives. It was inspired by a true incident when the author was about 19.

But let Vicky tell you about Summer Dreams:

I was David, but now I'm Vicky.

I was sunbathing in sand dunes near Bournemouth in 2003, when Roger found me and changed my life. After spending a heavenly holiday with him as Vicky, I just couldn't face reverting to David. I knew, though, that becoming Vicky permanently was impossible.

There was only one option, I tried to kill myself.

Roger saved me then showed how life as Vicky was possible.

But is it too good to last?

What other readers have said:

"Brilliant"

"LGBT meets Howard's Way*"

"A page turner"

"Informs about trans issues without pushing it down the readers throat"

"It's a really good introduction to transgender issues and a romantic novel very well written"

"It's proper steamy"

"John didn't put it down beginning of lockdown, kept saying his glasses were steaming up"

"I really liked how Vicky was kind, caring and non-judgmental. Even though she's lucky, she still offers her help to Mia. Even though things seem to go smoothly, the book still shows the after thoughts and insecurities."

"An interesting viewpoint in the life of someone transgendered, the difficulties faced in life, and also in transition, many of which I had not considered. The basic storyline is sound, though I did find it a little 'wordy' in places, especially with the smaller details in regards to sailing, flying, and of routes to various places which seemed unnecessary to the story. Having lived in and around Southampton for 45 years I did enjoy, and imagined precisely, descriptions of pubs and places and I have been to. A good effort though for a first novel."

"Romance ... and some sailing! This short novel follows Vicky as she falls in love with a man who seems too good to be true. But Vicky faces obstacles that you don't often read about in romance. She's a trans woman and we follow her through surgery, through the

Also by Helen Dale

process of coming out to her family, via various yachting incidents, right through to... well you'll have to read it to find out."

"Great characters, a compelling story and a healthy dose of realism. Helen Dale tells it like it is and you can't help cheering for Vicky in all her trials, hoping that she gets to live 'happily ever after'."

ISBN 978-1-9996329-3-9

Changes

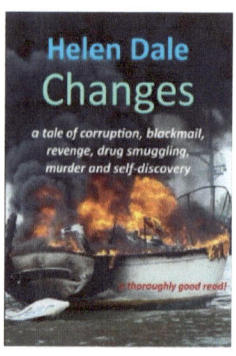

Changes is a tale of corruption, blackmail, revenge, drug smuggling, murder, and self-discovery told from five points of view:

Nigel Hall has a comfortable life running his advertising agency and using girls and other activities including sailing and trips to casinos to entertain his clients.

George Collins enjoys perks that Nigel gives him and doesn't worry too much about the invoices he approves.

John Ives hadn't expected to take his cousin **Carol Ives's** part as Cinderella in a panto when she injured her ankle horse-riding nor that photos from the event would later give his fiancée an idea for getting him in and out of her parents' house without their knowledge. Nor did he expect to discover how much he enjoyed cross-dressing or that his fiancée would support him.

Then **Mary Sanchez**, the widow of OJ, a former business partner of Nigel, returns from the USA. She takes over the company George works for and extracts revenge on Nigel, who she blames for OJ's death.

The consequences impact on all of them.

ISBN 978-1-9996329-6-0

Impact

Chris's family doesn't know he cross-dresses.

If his wife ever found out, it could be the end of his marriage — and cost him his daughter.

But CAN his activities remain secret?

If not, what will the impact be?

ISBN 978-1-7397667-1-9

Also by Helen Dale

Imposter

Jeff Shaw is transgender; he's been looking for a way of transitioning without causing financial problems for his family.

The train he's on is bombed and Michelle and Glen, two fellow passengers he's been talking to, are killed. Neither has family or friends to miss them and Jeff realises this is his opportunity for his male identity to be 'killed' in the incident and for him to reappear as Michelle.

But where did Michelle's substantial bank balance come from — and will it bring consequences in the future?

ISBN 978-1-7397667-2-6

Novella

Operation Busted Flush
a matter of survival

'"And I say the time for waiting is over. He's tried to stop us serving in the military. He's tried to withdraw rights we've fought for. He wants to prevent us using appropriate washrooms. Now he wants to eliminate us completely – they've even taken down every reference to transgender off government websites for Christ's sakes! Enough is enough. We have to f*****g do something!" Angela slapped her hand on the table.'

A group of ex-special forces transgender veterans decide to take action to defend their community against the White House's attack on transgender people.

As one reader said:

I want to see the movie of this book

Transgender avengers form a crack team to take down a corrupt and authoritarian US president before he causes more harm to their community. Good action-adventure romp with wish fulfilment for all those who have watched in despair over the past years as our hard won trans rights are attacked by governments worldwide. Thoroughly enjoyed it.

ISBN 978-1999632953

www.ingramcontent.com/pod-product-compliance
Lightning Source LLC
Chambersburg PA
CBHW040003110526
44587CB00006BA/151